A
LIFE OF LOVE

Dollipegs

Hope you enjoy

Love & Blessings
June Herrick
x

A
LIFE OF LOVE

Dollipegs

JUNE HERRICK

First published in Great Britain in 2018 by:
DAISA & CO
Westfield Lakes, Far Ings Road, Barton upon Humber
North Lincolnshire, DN18 5RG, England

Written by June Herrick
Copyright © June Herrick 2018

All material used for this book is from the Author's memory
and personal history. The editors have ensured a true reflection of the Author's tone
& voice have remained present throughout.
This book is a work of non-fiction based on the true life, recollections and experiences
of the author. In hoping to make the book more authentic, the author has named
everyone truthfully. The author wishes to express her apologies for any unintentional
embarrassment or offence caused and wishes to express her deepest respect for all
mentioned.

ISBN 978 1 9164928 0 6

A CIP catalogue record for this book is available from the British Library.

Book typeset by:
DAISA & CO
www.daisa-co.com

Printed in England

This book is made from paper certified by the Forestry Stewardship Council (FSC).
An organisation dedicated to promoting responsible management of forest resources.

Dedication

A special tribute to my Mam and Dad,
without them this story wouldn't have been possible.

I remember them with much love and affection.

Contents

Introduction

My name is June. I was born June Daulton, just before the War in 1937 in Grimsby, to Doris and Herbert Daulton, being the youngest of 4. My school days were at Welholme School until I left at the age of 15 in 1952.

When I was 20 years old, I married Raymond Herrick. Over 60 years later, we are still in love and have been blessed with two daughters and three grandchildren.

This is my story, a collection of memories from my life that I decided to write for me and my family; special memories that span a lifetime - a mixture of humour, laughs and naughty times.

'Dollipegs' - that's me!

It is the nickname I have endured for many years, I assume because I was so small and skinny... it just stuck!

I loved playing with Dolly Pegs and I used to have a shoe box with pillows and blankets to put my Dolly Pegs in... To me they were my babies.

Bill, Derrick, Gordon & June
My lips were so tight, so I didn't giggle, Gordon was nipping my shoulder
to make me laugh! In them days, this was a serious studio photo.

2lb Bag of Sugar

It all started in the year 1937, when I was born on the 26th May. Apparently, I was the weight of a 2lb bag of sugar and my godparents, Uncle Sam and Aunt Holly, told me in later years that I fitted in the palm of my Uncle's hand. He said I looked like a monkey covered in black downy hair! I remember as a teenager, Mam telling me that my Dad, for so many weeks, massaged and bathed me in olive oil.

Now at the age of 80, I am blessed, to have lived the longest in my family.

My first memories I recall was from about the age of 2 or 3 years – being taken to the shops in a pushchair. At that time, we lived at 294 Welholme Road, where I was born. I was blessed with 3 brothers and I was the youngest of the family.

Geoffrey (Bill) was the eldest and was 9 years my senior. Derrick was 18 months younger than Bill. Gordon was 2 years younger than Derrick and I was 4 years younger than Gordon.

I was spoilt and loved, also treasured a lot.

Mam

Mam at age 56 (taken in the 50's)

Mam was a hardworking, loving Mother who gave her time to us all – without favour – and we were always kept clean and well fed, even though we were poor. (Like many other families were).

My Mam was a 'no-nonsense-Mam', with a loving, caring nature and was always there for us no matter what; she would go out of her way to help. When I say 'no-nonsense-Mam', I mean she was very firm, and when she said "no" she meant it and never went back on her word and never gave into our whims or wants. I remember her saying to us "I don't make promises, because then there is no disappointment," she always said, "wait and see."

Mam was always a good listener and never allowed us to go silent or go to our room in a paddy or huff. She always knew if something was bothering us and wouldn't let it go – until she sorted the problem out.

Mam & Me (aged 35 & 4)

Mam used to curl my hair every night in rags to make it look thicker, and I don't know why, but she used to call me 'Eliza's come to stay', when I had rags in my hair.

Mam was very good at needle work and crochet and she taught me a lot. I used to love to sit beside her as she showed me. I remember she showed me how to make pleats. A lady down Convamore Road, called Mrs Major, would often give Mam snipping's of material that she had finished with. Mam would take them to the church to the Sewing Guild to make items to sell or use, perhaps making bits for the concerts too.

Mrs Major was a dress maker and she would make me dresses sometimes out of the remnants of material and used to put two pockets in the shape of cornets. I used to love them and felt quite posh. Mrs Major used to do her work in her front room; it was very messy. You couldn't see the carpet for cuttings of material! She was a lovely lady and so quietly spoken.

I recall on rare occasions, we used to have fizzy lemonade. Mam always put a few grains of sugar in it, because we didn't like the bubbles coming up on our faces. Perhaps it was because we were used to having drinks made out of lemons or lemon powder? Even to this day, I prefer to let the fizz go, before I enjoy it, but I must add, I don't think to put a little sugar into it!

A poem Mam taught me which is very special to me:

> *"The Company Lady wears a hat on her head*
> *My Mamma only has hair*
> *The Company Lady always wears gloves*
> *My Mamma's hands are bare*
> *In Winter, the Company Lady always wears fur*
> *In Summer, a chain of gold*
> *And everyone speaks kindly to her*
> *And her dresses are never old*
> *One day I broke one of Mamma's best cups*
> *She shook me and made my teeth chatter*
> *But when the Company Lady broke one*
> *She said, "Oh, it doesn't really matter"*

It is said your parents are always with you, and it is so true!

During our married life, we needed her help and she would stay for many weeks. In fact, my husband Ray, gave Mam a temporary job as a cleaner, at the school where he worked (which she loved) and also gave us great comfort at that time. She even taught Ray how to crochet and he made himself a woolly hat for which he was proud. Mam was very easy going and could take a joke, but certainly would fight her corner if she knew she was right.

Memories, mannerisms, the things I say and do daily are just like my Mam, through and through. Ray remarks and often says in a humorous way, "Don't look at me like your Mother."

Ray thought the world of my Mam, as she did about him.

She was a caring, loving Nanna to our 2 children, Julie and Lisa and was always pleased to help, nothing would be too much trouble.

We used to take the 'mickey' sometimes, when we took Mam on holiday and Julie was one for playing tricks on 'Nanna'.

One particular time, we were staying at a Guest House in Mablethorpe having our dinner and unbeknown to myself and Ray – Julie had placed a 'joke' bubble underneath 'Nanna's' plate; and when Mam was having her meal, Julie inflated the balloon from a lead out of sight and Mam thought her eyes were playing up! She was taking her glasses off, rubbing her eyes and putting her glasses back on again – picking up her spoon to have some soup, only to be confronted with a wobbly plate again... By this time, we were all in a state of giggles!

Then she realised and joined in with the laughter.

Julie also had a Whoopee Cushion which was great fun. Mam was always a good sport.

Dad

Dad at age 36 (taken in the RAF)

When we were young, we weren't allowed to speak at the table and this one time, one of us, I expect it would be Gordon, 'piped up'!

Dad tapped us all on the head with a tablespoon.

"What was that for Dad? We haven't done anything!"

Clonk. "There's another one for asking." Came the reply from Dad.

It never hurt and didn't do us any harm. In fact, we got to expect it, as Gordon would forget, and start talking. Dad used to say, "every time you speak, you miss a mouthful."

One time I remember, I hadn't been very well, so Dad made me wafer thin bread with condensed milk on, I loved it! I believe it helped to get my appetite back.

Dad was in the Royal Air Force at Warrington and I can still remember his number; 1476098 AC Squadron. When he came home on leave while in the RAF, he would jump off the train when it slowed down at Welholme Road junction. We used to stand at the front of our house and wait for his distant figure come into view (so much like in the film of the railway children). We were so excited and then there were times, when I was older courting my boyfriend (now my husband), meeting him at the station. The sound of the click of the doors and windows gave a rush of excitement and emotion at seeing him at the window ready to get off; such wonderful memories.

Then there were tears when he had to go back; waving goodbye as he leaned out of the window. I don't know how long Dad was in the forces, because he was also in the ARP (Air Raid Precautions).

A Present to Cherish

On my birthday, my Dad and I went down Heneage Road, to a shop called Byatts, a store that sold bits and bobs and hardware. In the window was a lovely green purse which he bought me and put a 6^d piece in. I was so fussy with it and I have still got it today.

Inside I have kept a few treasures from over the years. One of which is a small square box, with some silver threepenny pieces. Dad was going to make me a bracelet but never did get it finished. I have a lump of coal, a flattened penny that was squashed on the railway line, and a necklace made from ivory (all little elephants), which Uncle Horace brought back from India after the war.

I wore that on my Wedding Day.

I also have a letter which I wrote to my Dad in hospital. I remember him with much love and affection.

After the war, when Dad was working as a Barber, he would bring a couple of comics home for us. My favourite was 'The Knockout' and the boys had the 'Beano' and 'Dandy'. He worked for Mr Cowham in Part Street and Mrs Cowham ran the Ladies' Hairdressers. If I remember rightly, it was a double fronted shop, with the Ladies' Hairdressers at the back.

Mr and Mrs Cowham were very kind and understanding to Mam during Dad's illness and she received a lovely letter from them, when Dad passed away, which I still have.

Dad's Hat Took Off

My Dad always wore his trilby hat. On his way home from work, he would touch and slightly raise his hat to people that would be looking out the window, peeping around the curtain.

There was a lady who lived down Welholme Road not very far from us. She was rather nosy, or just lonely, I wasn't sure. Anyway, whether it was judgement on him, one day a gust of wind blew his hat off and he never did get it back, so that was an expense he could have done without.

~

I remember Dad getting Bronchitis quite a lot and after the war, he started to be poorly and had the odd time off work. Mam nursed him for quite a long time. I remember him going into hospital for tests and later found they couldn't do anything to make him better and he did suffer dreadfully.

These times are still so vivid in my mind, even after all these years. Dad was only 43 when he passed away, on January 8th 1949. Doctors had found a cancer which had spread to his brain.

Towards the end, Dad had to go into hospital and in them days, you were very much on your own. I often wondered how Mam had coped having three boys and myself to look after.

~

When I was in my early teens, Mam told me that my Dad came to his normal self shortly before he passed away and asked Mam to say the General Thanksgiving with him.

I feel that was a true belief in faith and love with our Saviour Jesus Christ, for all the suffering my Dad had to bear, and I am so grateful for my Mam sharing that with me.

School Days

I started school when I was five and fortunately didn't have far to go, we just had to cross the road from my house in Welholme Road and it took a five-minute walk to Welholme Infants.

First Day at School

I remember my first day at school very vividly. Miss Beeson was the Headmistress; she seemed very nice, but in them days, teachers always looked very stern. They seem much more approachable now.

Perhaps I wasn't very impressed with school, because on my first day, at playtime, I decided I wanted to go home and see my Mam, so off I went and trotted home… and Mam greeted me at the door with, "What are you doing coming home?!"

I had a rude awakening as she said, "You don't come home until dinner time!" She was quite cross and marched me straight back to school.

After that incident I had to sit by the side of Miss Ranns, my teacher, until it was time for Mam to pick me up.

I settled down after that episode. I knew I wasn't going to win.

June & her classmates at school

Margaret Rose

At school, there was a beautiful wendy house, very well equipped with a sand pit, a see-saw and a shop. I loved playing in the wendy house and especially pretending to be a mother with the dolls' pram. I wasn't lucky enough to have a dolls' pram at home until I was older, even then it was a tin one, but I loved it.

There was a girl named Elaine that lived a few doors away from me who had a lovely Silver Cross dolls' pram, nice covers, and a doll with sleeping eyes. My doll had a rag body with arms and legs made from a mixed material and pot. I remember going to Woolworths with my Dad to buy it; I was so excited and really treasured it.

I named my doll Margaret Rose after Princess Margaret. When Elaine and I played together, she let me walk her doll and pram back and forth up the garden path, but never allowed me to take the doll out of the pram. Sometimes she would attach the sun canopy and roll down the waterproof cover. I was so intrigued; it was a pleasure for me just to wheel it.

Kingfisher

I remember at school making a cardboard cut-out of a kingfisher, when I was about 6. The teacher cut it out for me; it was about 7 inches long and we had to stick a nipper peg on the back and the front was coloured in with wax crayons. When it was complete I was so proud of it. It soon took pride of place on the Christmas tree.

My Aunt Lizzie saw it on the tree and fell in love with it. She offered me 6^d for it which was a lot of money in those days to a little girl.

But I said, "No Aunty."

I treasured my Kingfisher for many years. I have often thought of making another one, but it wouldn't feel the same.

A Kingfisher drawing by June, aged 80

~

We'd have milk at school and the teacher would put it near the radiator – I hated it. (I much preferred cold milk with the cream frozen on the top, but it was never like that at school.)

When I was about 8 years old, Mrs Meggitt was my school teacher and she was very nice; she taught arithmetic. I always got top marks for mental arithmetic. I enjoyed English too and I nearly always achieved good marks for spelling, although I was often told my work was untidy.

I struggled with History and Geography. I enjoyed knitting and sewing; I remember making a pair of scarlet double knitting wool socks at the age of 10. I did wear them for a short time, but the rib stretched, and it made my skinny legs look even skinnier as they were baggy around my ankles!

During the war we hadn't much money although at the time, us kids didn't realise of course, because most people were in the same position. I remember going to school with newspaper in my shoes, which helped to keep my feet warm.

When I had a new pair of shoes, my Dad used to put metal segs on the tips of the soles and heels, to make them last longer. But I used to hate it because they made a clomping noise as I walked.

~

On Sports Day at school, we used to walk to the fields down Ladysmith Road.

This one particular day, I was eating some chewing gum ('Spoggy' we called it) whilst playing netball. Unfortunately, I bit my tongue and it started to bleed, so the teacher told me to nip my tongue until it stopped bleeding; it didn't last long. The teacher never found out that it was because I was chewing gum!

We always used to stick chewing gum on the bed post at night, ready to eat the next day; until we got fed up of it. Just like you hear in the songs,

'Does you chewing gum lose its flavour on the bed post overnight…'

I used to wish the walls were made up of packets of Beach Nut chewing gum, so I could take a packet, and more would come. Imagine that!

Miss Prim

I would sometimes try and get out of History and Geography lessons – I would be on the toilet outside at home, whether it was freezing or not and hoping I'd be late for school saying to Mam, "I've got a tummy ache." I used any excuse!
But Mam soon got wise to it, and put a stop to that, saying, "You will still go to school even if you are late. So, you had better get a move on!"

My Mam never stood any nonsense, "And you can change that face as soon as you like Miss Prim!"

Proper Mess

I remember contracting impetigo once; I looked a proper mess. I had to have purple liquid dabbed on my face and arms which was called Gentian Violets. I even had to go to school like it.

June aged 11

Caning

During the last few months at school, I had my first and last caning. It was a miserable and wet day. At playtime we were asked by a Prefect to go outside. There were about 12 of us sitting in the cloak room and we all decided we weren't going out. We said, "let us stay in."

The Prefect reported us, and we were all called to the Headteacher's Office and given 2 strokes of the cane – one on each hand.

Feathers

Derrick had a friend called Terry at school, who was always very kind and nice to me. He always called me 'Smiler'.

One day, we were asked to bring a feather to class to use as a quill (well I never liked feathers and even now I wouldn't have a feather pillow or cushions!) So, I gingerly held the feather and tightly because I didn't want it to move.

On the way to school, Terry noticed I wasn't very happy. So, he kindly walked with me to the gate, but I managed to keep my cool... Phew! What an experience!

I also used to have a phobia for birds and butterflies but thankfully, I have overcome those now – almost!

Letters to Film Stars

When I was about 13 years old, there was a craze of collecting film star photos and at the same time, Eileen and myself used to pretend we were film stars (Eileen acted as Patricia Roc because she was blonde, and I played Judy Garland as I had dark hair).

We would send letters to Pinewood Studios requesting photos of the stars.

The letter would read…

> *'Dear Ava Gardner,*
> *Margaret Lockwood or Veronica Lake.*
> *Could you please send me a photograph of yourself, as*
> *you are one of my favourite film stars and I have always*
> *wanted a photograph of you.*
> *I would be obliged if you would send me one.*
> *Yours sincerely,*
> *June Daulton.'*

We did get one or two different photos but not always what we asked for. I remember getting one of Tommy Trinder, who wasn't my heart throb, but I was pleased to receive it.

During that time, Autograph Books were also popular. I had one but never had the opportunity to ask any celebrities, so mine was filled by friends and neighbours.

Potato Picking

A few of us girls decided we would like to go potato picking… So, we arranged it and one girl's father asked the telegraph reporter to come and take our photos, so they did.

The young volunteers photographed by The Grimsby Telegraph as they set out on one of their premature potato-picking expeditions. June pictured far right.

Caption from The Grimsby Telegraph:

"The young volunteers photographed as they set out on one of their premature potato-picking expeditions.

Thirteen-year-old Shirley Hopwood of Convamore Road, read in the Evening Telegraph that many acres of potatoes might be left to rot in the ground if casual workers did not help the farmers, so Shirley and her group of friends decided that potato picking was a good way to spend the summer holidays.

But they were too early, so Shirley's gang found a nice hedge, ate their sandwiches and drank their lemonade and counted buses taking holidaymakers to Cleethorpes.

The group included: Shirley Hopwood (13), David Parker (10), Hannah Curtis (9), Shirley Potterton (12), Barbara Horsewood (12) and June Daulton (11)."

But unfortunately, when we arrived at the fields we were told that they didn't need any more workers and we were a week too soon. We were so disappointed.

The Telegraph reporter had asked what we would have done with our money. I replied, "I was going to decide what to do with the money when I got it!"

Senior School

My first taste of a banana was at the beginning of Senior School. They were delivered in a long, wooden box and given to each child. On another occasion, we were also given drinking chocolate.

At school, I loved doing laundry and cooking lessons. The classes were in a separate block in the playground. The teacher was called Mrs Miller. She was a very small, well-built lady, only about 5ft tall. Mrs Miller always had a wooden spoon in her hand, ready to tap you one if things weren't right! She taught us some very good lessons which I still follow today!

One particularly good tip was to rinse the dish cloths out with cold water and regularly sterilise or boil in a pan. When we did the ironing, it was often done by a flat iron which was heated. We were very fortunate if we managed to get the chance to iron with an electric one. We used to test the heat by splashing it with water and if hot enough, it would sizzle.

Our art lessons were taken in an adjoining part of the same building. Our teacher was very nice, but I wasn't really into art in them days. However, my friend Eileen, showed promise.

Much later in life, I took art lessons with Lesley Treacher and enjoyed it very much. I also completed an art course at college.

Paper Round

I had a paper round at Cottingham's down Hainton Avenue, when I was 14 years old. I delivered the paper every weekday morning, evening and Saturday (Football Telegraph). I wasn't keen on working the Saturday but endured it. I was paid 10 shillings (50p). Half of my earnings went in the bank and I would go to the pictures once a week, then go for a Horlicks afterwards at the snack bar which was down Pasture Street and I still had enough left for a sweet or two!

My brother, Gordon, also had a paper round and he told Mam that at one of the houses he delivered to, there was a moth or butterfly the size of half a brick, inside the porch. Well of course, nobody believed him. So, I went with him the next time to see for myself. He didn't say where it was, he just said, "I'll tell you, you lass – when we get there." It wasn't until I was in the porch, that he showed me it, nestled in the corner.

I ran out so quickly; it really was the size of half a brick! Whilst I ran around the back (it was obvious they didn't use the front door) the lady came through from the back and opened the door which disturbed the creature and it flew away into the trees. Apparently, the homeowner phoned someone who came and caught it in a net. It seemed this bizarre creature had travelled from abroad!

Mary Mouse

I was never an avid reader in my school days but there was one series of books I loved; the stories of Mary Mouse by Enid Blyton.

Mary Mouse lived in a little dolls house in the basement with her husband and 6 children and looked after the Doll family and 3 children and not forgetting Jumpy the Dog. These stories were full of adventure and portrayed so much family love. I mentioned these stories to Julie, a few years ago and she presented me with two original books from the series. I was so thrilled. I sat and read them all over again…

'Here Comes Mary
Mouse Again'
– Book 2

'More Adventures of Mary
Mouse' – Book 6

Brotherly Love

Growing up with three brothers, Geoffrey (Bill), Derrick and Gordon, I was always going to be a bit of a Tom Boy!

I did hang around a lot with Gordon, following him and his friends and he used to say, "Clear off you lass." But I didn't take much notice.

Gordon was very much his own person, it was always 'you get what you see' with him and for that he was loved by many who knew him.

Gordon was a bit of a rebel at times, he also hated school. He wasn't a very good scholar and I often helped him with Arithmetic and English. However, as he matured, he was a lot better and caught up in every aspect of his education.

When he came home from school his socks were always ruffled to his ankles and one could always tell what he had used his sleeves for! Mam used to say, "You look as though you don't belong to anyone!" And yet, when he started work and going out with his mates, there wasn't a smarter lad. In fact, they were all very smartly dressed.

I remember the time when Gordon played truant for a whole 5 days. I knew; but said I wouldn't tell Mam. But of course, she soon got to know as in those days the school board man would come around to check why you hadn't been in school. Mam was so cross as she had no idea! He used to go and watch the trains at Peaks Field Tunnel. The only thing he enjoyed about school was woodwork or anything practical. He got by, and when he left school he started as a labourer, with Derrick as he was training to be a brick layer. Gordon joined him until it was call up time for National Service when he was eighteen.

Derrick joined later, when he was 21, after he finished his apprenticeship. Both Derrick and Gordon went in the RAOC (Royal Army Ordnance Corps) and Bill went into The Royal Engineers when he was 21, after finishing his apprenticeship in Constructional Engineering.

Derrick is a Film Star

Derrick loved acting and when he was younger, he starred in quite a few plays, held at All Saints Church, until he went in the Army. I used to help him with his lines as he always had a main part.

I remember one play he was in. I was sitting in the front row and I heard a voice behind me say,

"Who does that man remind you of… Some film star?" someone replied saying, "Trevor Howard!"

Derrick certainly shared a resemblance when he was young, especially in the film, 'Brief Encounter' – Derrick looked just like him.

A few years ago, my daughter Lisa and her husband Ian bought me the film for Christmas. A very bittersweet feeling as my brother is no longer with us; it was a long time before I felt I could watch it.

Potions

I remember when I was about 10, when Mam and Dad went out of an evening (which wasn't very often) I was left at home with Derrick and Gordon. We would get all sorts out of the pantry like salt, flower, baking powder, Andrews Liver Salts, sugar and vinegar – anything we could lay our hands on! We would take it in turns to make up these potions, and the others would be blind folded. It was a wonder we weren't sick with the concoctions we made up! But we always had a good laugh, and all was put away before Mam and Dad came home. Mind you, one incident we were playing 'doctors' and Gordon got a chair and went into the pantry and reached for Dad's cut throat razor off the top shelf. Dad always said never play with the razor, but Gordon being mischievous had to try it... on me... yes me! He decided to shave my hairs off my arms as I had quite a lot of dark hair and on doing so, nipped my arm and made it bleed.

"Oh Gordon! You'll get into trouble when Mam and Dad come home." I said.

He replied, "Don't tell them you lass."

But of course, there was no chance of hiding the accident as I had to have a bandage on my arm. We always had a first aid box handy so of course, when Mam and Dad came home and saw the bandage they wanted to know what had been going on! So, Gordon ended up with a big telling off. That was the first and *last* time the razor was played with.

The Forgotten Wave Clip

There was a shop on the corner called Hector Jackson...

One day when Gordon was about 17, he let me put a wave in his hair. I did this by using a wave clip. A short time later, he went to Hector's to buy something and there were a few customers in the shop and he wondered why they all looked at him. Until he realized - he had forgotten he still had the clip in his hair!

He came back and said, "You lass, why didn't you tell me I'd still got the wave clip in!?"

Me! I always got the blame. Mam and I had a good laugh about that... Gordon didn't see the funny side.

Gordon aged 9

~

Now Derrick, he was always clean and tidy, although he did get into some scrapes. He was far from perfect, always fighting - mainly defending his friends.

Derrick aged 10

One day a knock came at the door and there was a boy saying that Derrick was tied to a tree and was being stoned, just like Jesus! Mam ran out and untied him, the kids ran off, but his nose was pouring with blood.

Then on another occasion he ended up in hospital after he'd had an unfortunate accident with a pitch fork after the kids dared him to use his foot as a target!

At 11 or 12, Derrick was climbing the metal railings at the Gaiety, topped with spikes; he slipped and was impaled by the spikes in his arm pit.

Geoffrey (Bill) aged 12

Bill, my eldest brother, was always known as the 'Rev' because he was very smart, studious and wore spectacles.

He had five rabbits that he cared for and looked after along with other animals. Mam once told me (when I got older) that when Bill was two years old, she caught him feeding baby Derrick sultanas!

Scrumping
'Scrump' – to take fruit from an orchard or garden.

Times were full of devilment and sometimes we even went 'Scrumping'. We always found something to do.

I would be allowed to go 'Scrumping' with Gordon and his friends but only because he needed me to be on the lookout...

One day, I was distracted and not paying attention and the boys were caught in the act – up an apple tree! An old man came out waving his stick at them. They certainly came down quicker than they went up!

Afterwards, I got a punch on my arm from Gordon, he said, "You're not coming with us anymore you lass!" But of course, I did!

There was a house on Weelsby Road, near 'People's Park', on the corner of Park Avenue, that had an apple tree over hanging by the fence, which was great as they were quite easy to get to. We would fill our pockets and dash across to the park, sit on the grass and munch away. The only thing was they weren't ripe enough for eating and we all wondered why we'd got belly aches the next day. There wasn't any sympathy from my Mam; "You'll learn," she'd say.

~

There was a time when 'Go Karting' was all the craze (around 1948) and Gordon decided to build his own Go-Kart. He had 2 sets of wheels with a plank of wood on top for the seat and it could be steered by string, which was attached to the front wheels.

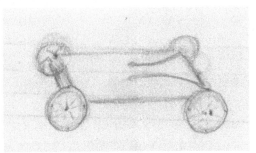

Sketch of similar 'Go Kart' by June

Well, you can imagine what came next!

My brother said, "You can have a go first you lass." Lo and behold, I was all for it!

He shouted, "get on then and I'll give you a push; hold onto the string to steer it!" He gave me a big push and the wheels drifted and I went flying... Grazing all down my leg and I went to show my Mam (hoping Gordon would get into trouble, but no!) All I got from Mam was, "you should have more sense," and told me to get it washed. I was only about 10 years old at the time, but I was tough.

~

At that age, I also went to Acro and Tap Dancing. I was in Pauline Nurses' garden; four doors away with a few friends and because I was the 'weeny' one (the other kids were all a couple of years older than me) we did a pyramid: 3-2-1. I was the one on top doing the splits. Mam came out and nearly had a fit!

"Get down, you'll be hurting yourself!"

It's a wonder I didn't fall off when she shouted. I never saw the danger, I was having fun. I remember saying, "I'm alright Mam."

She was still worried saying, "Anyway get down." So, I had to do as I was told. Eh!

~

I do remember on one occasion, going to the fields at the back of Old Clee church with Gordon and his mates. It was a bit hilly there and we used to naughtily watch the courting couples having a cuddle on the grass (it's called 'snogging' these days!) If they caught us looking at them, we used to run away laughing. It was all good fun though; in those days, we never got bored.

Our pleasures were very simple; we would have great fun just with a cycle wheel, taking it in turns to roll it down the hill, near where the chapel is on Welholme Road and Convamore Road.

A Policeman came to Call

We, as a family, were full of mischief and if we stepped over the line - it would be the one and only time. My Mam had a cane above the door and if she picked that up the boys knew Mam meant it and backed away. It was never used.

I remember one time, Derrick got into trouble. He would've been about 12 and we would run down the passages at the back of the houses, doing no harm and there was a lady that came out, moaning at us; telling us to clear off.

We called her Old Ma Loftis. One time, our Derrick spat on her shed and Dad heard of the incident. So, he asked the local policeman to call.

I remember the drama so clearly;

A knock came at the door. Dad said, "Derrick go and see who that is." when he opened it, there stood a policeman. By this time, the rest of us were being nosey, standing at the living room door, Dad standing behind Derrick...

"Do you have a boy named Derrick?" The policeman asked.

Dad said, "Yes here he is." pointing to Derrick.

"Now then sonny, I hear you've been spitting on a lady's shed up the road?"

Derrick looked so sheepish and scared, stepping back.

The policeman looked at him sternly and said, "If you promise me you'll be a good lad, no more spitting, no more will be said about it."

So, Derrick promised, and all was well, but it frightened him so much that he never spat again.

This never stopped us running down the passages and Ma Loftis was always there to have a moan.

Grandmothers

Grandma Daulton & Grandma Weatherall

My two Grandmothers were so different. Grandma Daulton was very generous but wasn't very fair at times. She spoilt my eldest brother; my Mam said it was because he was so much like

Uncle Joseph, who was killed during WW1. There was perhaps a special bond, he was also her first grandchild. I learnt as I got older, that Derrick was never in favour with Grandma Daulton, which made my Mam cross.

Grandma Daulton, Gordon & Derrick

Now, Grandma Weatherall, didn't spoil any of us but was a very fair lady and never suffered fools gladly. Both Grandmas were very smart.

They were always wearing black or navy; Grandma Weatherall especially loved a navy pinstripe. Her son, my Uncle Alf from Boston, used to keep her well-dressed, because he was a tailor.

We rarely saw Grandma Weatherall without her hat indoors or out (except at bedtime of course!) Even then, she always wore a turban type cover which we never questioned, we just accepted it.

I remember Derrick would flip her hat from the back and say, "Hello Grandma" and she would get cross.

Although Grandma expected Derrick to tip her hat he was so quick and sharp with his eyes he caught Grandma every time when she wasn't thinking about it and she used to say, "Damn your eyes and God forgive me for saying such a thing!"

Derrick was full of devilment and would often wind Grandma up.

I realised, as I got older, Grandma Weatherall wore her hat a lot because she had very little hair. (Dinky curlers were used, and she just had three. One at the top of her head and one either side and when she took her curlers out she would fluff her hair up – just like back combing.)

At birthdays, she never gave out birthday cards, saying they were a waste of money. So, she always gave us a 3^d bit.

At Christmas, it would be a 6^d piece. Then we did think we were well off!

The two Grandmas lived in the same house, in separate rooms, in Torrington Street. Grandma Weatherall had the front room, which consisted of a sink, an open fireplace, two fireside chairs and a three-quarter sized bed and a table the size of a card table, two chairs and a kitchenette unit, chest of drawers. She used the door for hanging her clothes.

Grandma Daulton's room had a double bed, chest of drawers, wardrobe and one easy chair. She also had the use of the kitchen with Cissy Mortlock.

There was also a small rocking-chair, which I loved, and Grandma promised me I could have it when I was older and when she passed away, it was given to me and I have treasured it, to this day.

When I nursed my babies, it was used for bathing them and cuddles, but unfortunately, now I can't fit my bottom in it - I was skinny in them days!

I have often wondered why Grandma Weatherall came to Grimsby from Burgh-le-

Marsh. I feel sad that I didn't get to know more about it from my Mam, because she also lived for a short time down Peaks Field Avenue – not far from where my Aunt Lizzie used to live.

I used to stay over at a weekend because I remember going to school from Grandma's. I loved spending time with her and we used to sew or mend things and darn socks. We used to have a shaped mushroom stool that would go inside a sock so to hold the sock tight while it was being repaired.

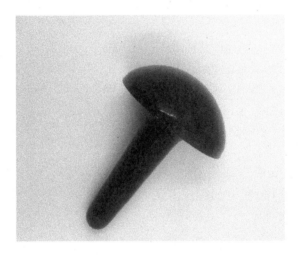

I never liked using a thimble, but Grandma insisted. Especially if the needle had to go through thick material. I loved doing blanket stitch, which was used for edging blankets and that needle was called a 'cruel needle'.

On Guy Fawkes Day Grandma Daulton, always bought the fireworks, as it was her birthday she used to treat us. She never went outside though, she preferred to stay indoors and look out the window. She always liked me to sit by her side. Mind you, I didn't care for the jumping jacks as you never knew where they were going to end up.

~

Sadly, after Dad passed away, Grandma Daulton (his mother) took to her bed. She came to visit one afternoon after Dad's funeral and her speech wasn't very good; saying things that didn't relate to anything. Mam made a cup of tea and Grandma said her foot hurt. I remember Mam suggesting she take her shoe off. When she did Mam noticed a big safety pin in her stockings, so she knew something was amiss, because Grandma was such a proud lady – she would never have let that happen.

Grandma Daulton passed away on February 8th and it was said she died of a broken heart.

294

Welholme Road

Our home was very simply furnished. Our kitchen consisted of a deep, white sink and one kitchen table which Mam scrubbed regularly – that's where we did the washing up in a bowl on the table. On the other side, opposite the sink, there was a wash copper boiler which had to be filled with water, with a fire underneath; this would heat the water. A dolly tub and dolly peg were kept on top when not in use.

To the right there was the coal house where the coal and wood were stored. The Coal Man had to come inside the kitchen to deposit the coal. There was also a small fireplace which wasn't used as we couldn't afford it and the gas cooker stood near a clothes horse and a big pantry.

The mangle was left outside under waterproof sheeting. We used to build a tent, outside or inside, using the clothes horse – such fond memories!

We loved playing in the tent; Mam used to let us have a draped sheet over the clothes horse. We even used to be allowed to use the big table in the living room. Mam let us have some old curtains and she threaded them with string or tape, so they would rest on top of the table. Just sitting round the edge and we even used to have a little torch hanging so we could see at night.

Very happy times!

I was allowed one friend over to play at a time. On occasion, Gordon would come creeping in, but he didn't stay for long. He was only being nosy or wanted to annoy me.

~

We had an outside toilet with a big wooden seat. In those days, we couldn't afford toilet paper (most people were the same) so we would cut up newspaper into squares, of about 8 inches with string slotted through to hang on the door on a nail. If we ever had oranges or new shoes, the tissue paper that they were wrapped was used instead - this was a luxury, (a bit slippery though!)

The only time I sampled Izal toilet roll was when I went and stayed with my Aunt May and Uncle Alf in Boston; I loved the smell of it.

During the winter months, I never liked going outside at night to the toilet because it was so dark and creepy but Mam always insisted.

She'd stand at the back door and say, "Don't be long…"

If it all went quiet, I'd call out nervously, "Are you still there?"

She'd shout back, "I won't be if you don't hurry up!" Bless her.

~

Shopping Lists

Mam used to do her shopping at 'Hotson's' on the corner of Welholme Road and Heneage Road.

When I was almost 9 years old, jam jars were saved up, and exchanged for a $\frac{1}{2}^d$ or 1^d each; and when a few had been collected I would take them back to the shop and Mr Hotson always used to say, "Oh! Resurrection Day today."

He was a very nice gentleman and always kind and helpful to my Mam. Of course, in those days groceries were paid for at the end of the week, as most people used to run up an account until Friday; when the bread winner brought their wage home (in them days, this was usually the Father figure in the house).

I loved going into 'Hotson's' and was fascinated by the big, 'Bacon Machine'. It was red with a very large sharp blade; it never occurred to me that one day I would be using one. This would be when I started my first job at the age of 15, in the year 1952.

As a family, we hadn't got much money and Dad after the War, would only bring home a few pounds as he was a Barber with a very low wage. He would have to rely on tips from his customers, which weren't plentiful.

I remember occasionally, he would bring home some chocolate given to him by a customer, when the fishing boats came in. Thinking back, it tasted awful, but I enjoyed it at the time as Mam and Dad were unable to get our sweet ration allowance regularly.

~

Opposite our house, there was the corner grocery shop, that belonged to Hector Jackson.

He was a very obliging man and worked very hard; it was a family business and his father run it until he passed away. His Dad was a very smart man, he used his carrier bike for taking groceries round to his customers.

We could see straight into his house from our bedroom window and he always had a newspaper on the table. People would knock on the door when he had closed for something they had forgotten, and he never refused them. He never invited them in though, they always had to wait outside.

~

There was Miss Tuplin's shop that was like a little treasure chest, with an aroma from it which always seemed to be very inviting. A sweetness of biscuits and sweets when you walked in.

If there were no customers, you wouldn't be able to see Miss Tuplin as the counters were stacked so high! The only space was the smallest of counters with a lift-up lid and gate to enable her to come out and serve vegetables. She was a very pleasant lady.

If you couldn't get what you needed from Miss Tuplin's (then you'd had it!) other than going to the Freeman Street Market.

I liked those little liquorice sweets; they were named 'Nipits', no bigger than. Sometimes when I played 'Mother' and having a baby, I would pretend the 'Nipits' were tablets to take from the doctors.

~

I was a skinny little thing and I had a poor appetite; I don't think the war time helped. I loved the stews that Mam made. They used to last a few days and were made with marrowbones and we always had dumplings.

When we were getting towards the end of a jar of jam, we took it in turns to clean the jar out. Mam would give us a fork and some squares of crusts of bread and we all loved that!

Apples & Lost Handkerchiefs

Mam told me many years ago that when her sister was a young girl, if she saw who she thought was a posh, clean lady or gentleman eating an apple walking down the street, she would follow until the person dropped the core. She would then pick it up and eat it!

When I was young, Mam would bring a stray handkerchief home, which she had found, soak it in salt water, then boil it up in a special pan she used to have for smalls.

It was just what we did in those days…

Waste not, want not.

There's Always Room for Pudding

When Mam made rice pudding, she'd cook it in the side oven of the fireplace and it would have a lovely, brown skin with a sprinkling of nutmeg. When finishing the pudding, we'd all take turns and scrape round the edges. It always tasted extra special!

Mam used to make lovely spotted dick pudding which tasted yummy. It was made with sultanas, flour, suet, and sugar – mixed and poured into a dish and covered. Or, put in a muslin rag and then steamed for a couple of hours.

We also enjoyed Jam Roly-Poly. Again, the dough was made with suet and rolled out, covered in jam and then rolled up like a Swiss Roll and baked in the oven. Always served with custard! Absolutely delicious (this pudding would be made after the war!)

I loved banana and custard. Mam would cut the banana up soaking them in custard. That was very tasty! I still enjoy a banana every day; half with my breakfast and the other with my supper; along with any other fruit prepared by my husband. He is good!

Toast was another firm favourite in our family, especially in the winter around the fire. We used a long toasting fork, the prongs went through the bread and we toasted it on top of the fire. Or we could have French toast (one sided) or beef dripping (Lard was best if there was no dripping) on toast then sprinkled with salt…delicious!

My Dad loved tripe... Yuck! That *really* used to make me feel sick! It was poached in milk. I refused to try it.

"Come on Spadge, try it!" He'd say. (He always called me Spadge, which meant Sparrow).

Lemonade

Sometimes in the summer, Mam would have a glass jug of lemon juice sitting in the pantry, so if we were thirsty we could take a drink. But we had strict orders to drink it sparingly, as it had to go around - in other words, serve the four of us.

I don't think Mam often got a look in!

I use the same glass jug at the table today. It was always made with fresh lemons with the pieces floating in the water and Mam would keep topping it up with more water and sugar. After a while the flavour would be gone, but we didn't complain.

I'm afraid in those days; you had to take what was given or do without.

Chores

As I got older, Mam had me cleaning the front porch and window sills. She said, "I think it's about time you learnt a few household chores..."

Those days, people were very proud of the appearance of their fronts…

I remember Mrs Horsewood, who lived across the road from us, used to get on her hands and knees and she'd scrub from the gate to the porch; it was all shiny tiles and everywhere looked spotless.

Well, going back to my chores, Mam gave me a bucket of water and the step stone and showed me what to do.

The step stone was used for whitening the door step and window ledges and I had to clean the tiles with some nice hot water and then when it was dry, I had to cardinal polish it, which was red and it made the tiles look bright and shiny. Mam use to come out while I was on my knees.

"Make sure you don't leave it all 'smeary'."

I used to do a fair bit of huffing and puffing with a sigh, to say the least.

On occasion, I had to black lead the fire grate in the living room and had to make sure it was done properly. We hadn't got much but there was a sense of pride to look after what you had.

~

When I was young, sometimes I used to help Barbara, from next door. She used to do braiding at home, making fisherman's nets and I would go around and fill the shuttles and she would give me 2 shillings, which was a lot of money in them days.

Mam couldn't afford to give me pocket money. She did have a job at Smethurst's, which did become Birds Eye. At the time, when the pea lorries slowed down at the corner of Welholme Road and Convamore Road, Gordon and his mates used to pull some off as they were hanging down over the lorries enough to be able to reach.

I remember Gordon coming into Mam's kitchen with them. She was so cross! He didn't do it again however Mam did use them. In those days, we couldn't afford to turn away good food!

Fish in Newspaper

There wasn't much heating in our house, only in the living room and when we went to bed, Mam would give us a hot oven shelf with newspaper wrapped round it to warm the bed. For extra warmth, we'd use heavy army blankets which you could buy from the army and navy stores.

Mind you, I don't honestly know where ours came from. Most people had them so perhaps they were issued to us during the war?

And by the way - newspaper print didn't come off in those days.

We used to have fish and chips wrapped in newspaper from the fish shop. The fish shop was only just across the road from where we lived – 8 doors up – so it was handy. I don't think we had them very often until the 1950's. Uncle Sam, my godparent, used to work on the docks, and he would on occasion, bring some over and by 'eck they were delicious! Lovely and thick and pure white. Mam used to shallow-fry it. Just thinking about it makes my mouth water! We were very lucky in Grimsby as we had the best!

The first time Ray (my then boyfriend) came to Grimsby, Mam said we would have fish and chips from the shop, thinking it would be a nice treat for him, but he told us he wasn't keen on fish… Mam said, "I expect you haven't tasted good fish!"

So, he said he would try and guess what? Yes! He was converted immediately and has loved fish ever since! Only the best though.

Later in life when Ray and I went to visit his family in Birmingham, we would take some fresh Grimsby fish and we'd ask the fish shop proprietor in Birmingham if he would fry the fish for us… and we always gave him some skate. He had never seen it before. The family loved fresh fish from Grimsby.

Working for a Living

When I left school, I started work as an Assistant in a Grocery Shop in Park Street.

Mr and Mrs Smith were the proprietors and I loved working for them. Mrs Smith always did the baking on a Monday morning to sell in the shop and she would always give me a cake with my morning break. Unfortunately, after about 18 months they had to sell the business due to Mr Smith's ill health.

That's when Mr Smelt took it over. He was a completely different type of person to work with. He was trained at Tate's Supermarket and wanted me to work the same way; reminding the customer what they might need, so I used to have to say, "Are you alright for, butter – sugar – eggs – bread – milk – bacon?" and so on.

It was okay but after a while, I felt like a change. After working there for about a year, I moved on to work in Chelmsford Avenue Newsagents. Mr Ryder was a great boss; kind and generous and always thanked me for whatever I did and often rewarded me with an extra 2^s6^d or a bar of chocolate.

Unfortunately, though, when they had a new assistant from school things weren't so good, Mr Ryder was often poorly and Mrs Pullen (Mr Ryder's right hand) expected more from me. I had to take the young girl in hand which was very difficult as she didn't get the jobs done as expected. So, after about 6 months of the girl joining us, I left. I found out later that the girl left just after me.

~

I had another job as a Cost Clerk, which was temporary at Ticklers Jam Factory in Pasture Street.

After that I worked as a temp at Nickerson seed merchants as a telephonist on the PBX. I loved that job which lasted about 6 months.

My last job, before I got married and went to live in Birmingham, was a Shop Assistant in Farebrother Street; they too were great to work for and they bought me a pastry board and rolling pin as a wedding present.

Lather Up

The soap that was used quite a lot in those years was Life Buoy Soap (it had a nice, fresh smell) and green Fairy soap. One day, we hadn't any shampoo and my friend, Maureen said, "I sometimes use Oxydol wash powder." But she had medium-blonde, thick hair… Anyway, I had a go – oh! What a mess, me having black and very fine, it left deposits of white bits in my hair. So,

Mam had to give it a good rinse for me and wasn't very well pleased, as it meant boiling more water. At the time we hadn't running hot water, which wasn't available until 1960.

Resting

In the days when I was a young girl, when a person died they would be kept in a coffin in their own house which was the normal thing to do, if they had a spare room and friends and neighbours would pay their respects by viewing the body. When a loved one had passed on and was 'resting' in our front room, my Mam would leave a dim light on, all day and night, with the door slightly ajar. She used to say she didn't like them to be in the dark, alone. I remember her going in to my Dad often, talking to him, but she wouldn't allow me to go in as she wanted me to remember him as he was. I was tempted to peep but I thought '*best not*'.

Blinds were drawn in the area (out of respect) and when the funeral procession had passed then they would open them again. The wake was usually organised by a dear neighbour or friend, to come in and prepare the food. Caraway Seed Cake was very popular to give – and that is where the name came from, as 'Funeral Cake'.

Wash Days

Wash days were long days, the copper boiler would be put on early morning and everything was rinsed either in the deep white sink or was in a bucket under the outside tap and Mam would douche them up and down "like that there…" one of Mam's sayings – we used to laugh about it, because when she was explaining how to do something – she used to say, "Like that there."

Ha! Ha! Happy memories.

'Reckitt's Blue Bag' was used for the whites – for the final douche, swish the Bag in clear water. Then put the white shirts in or whatever you wanted to look extra white after they had, had a boil.

Mam was very proud of her washing, as were a lot of people those days.

There was one time, when it was washing day, Mam felt sure there was a mouse in the dolly tub where Mam kept the dirty washing, so she asked me to tip the soiled clothes out and there it was! I had the hand shovel at the ready and hit it once. We used to have quite a lot of mice around, even holes in the skirting boards.

Sundays are for Church

Every Sunday morning, afternoon and evening, we went to church as a family. We didn't always go to three services, but we were very involved with the church. I enjoyed going and watching my three brothers, who were all in the choir. My Dad always performed 'side duty'.

I loved sitting in the front row, as I used to have a soft spot for one of the boys. I used to call him Clanky Clarke. He belonged to the Church Lads Brigade and my Dad was the Lieutenant. I was a member of the Brownies and later the Girl Guides. I loved taking part in the church parades, once a month.

There were lots of activities going on at All Saints Church. The church had quite a large hall and not only did they use it for C.L.B and Guides etc. but there was a youth club/sewing guild, which Mam belonged to.

There were concerts and plays, performed in the Church Hall. Derrick was in quite a lot of plays, taking the main part. I was also involved in the productions, but usually dancing. So the parents had plenty of stage costumes to make.

~

The Girl Guides' inspection was very strict, every week, from top to toe. Tidy hair, hands and nails were essential; along with polished shoes and pressed uniform. One evening, we learned Morse Code which I loved.

I remember when I was in the Brownies, there was a special day in the People's Park and we were doing an activity about cleanliness. We each had a bowl and chair. The bowl was placed on the chair and we were given some water, a toothbrush and paste, flannel, soap and towel. Fortunately, it was a beautiful, warm day, as we were only in our vests and pants!

We all sang:

> *"Here we go 'round the mulberry bush*
> *The mulberry bush, the mulberry bush*
> *Here we go 'round the mulberry bush*
> *On a cold and frosty morning!*
>
> *This is the way we clean our teeth*
> *Clean our teeth, clean our teeth,*
> *This is the way we clean our teeth,*
> *On a cold and frosty morning!"*

Mam also belonged to the Young Wives' Fellowship, the Mother's Union and she belonged to the Ladies Choir. When it was the Coronation Year, choirs all over the country sang in the Albert Hall and met the Queen – Mam was so excited!

It helped a lot to get involved at the church and even more so after Dad passed away.

Our Sunday School outings and day trips were at Caistor Sandbraes and we used to have such great times. Mam would take our packing up, which was homemade lemonade, (made from Lemonade Crystals, or fresh lemons topped with water), beef dripping sandwiches and jam and cheese, if we were lucky.

~

We were all, in turn, confirmed; the boys had their confirmation whilst Dad was alive but mine was in 1950. By that time, the boys had drifted away from church, as most do when they grow up and find their own way, but I still feel that we had a good foundation and knew our boundaries - even if we were full of it! Always trying to push our luck…

As a Vicar once said, "Only sinners come to church, you don't have to be good. Those without sin cast the first stone."

Bus Hopping & Holidays

When I was young, about 9 years old, we would visit Burgh – Le – Marsh for a few days.

In those days, we did what one would call 'bus hopping' – changing buses at each village or small towns I.e. Grimsby – Louth – Spilsby – Boston – Spalding – Peterborough.

My Grandma Weatherall, Mam's mother, was a housekeeper for a farmer and we used to have great times on the farm. We would climb up the hay stacks and have tons of fun.

I loved carrying a candle upstairs to bed. The door to the stairs was in the living room and the steps were winding and steep. There was a chamber pot under the bed for during the night.

I can remember that the old man, on occasion, would throw its contents out of the window; shouting at the cats for making a lot of noise in the middle of the night!

He had a Lincolnshire accent;

"Bugger 'orf you yowling cats!"

~

There was another relation we used to visit, he was a dear old gentleman, small and portly built, little and dumpy.

We knew him as Uncle Ben. He was related to my Mam's side of the family but that is all I know. He was always a generous man and always gave us a 6^d piece to put in our pockets. I do remember him coming over to see us after the war but only once.

~

I also remember going to Peterborough with the family to see Aunt Nancy and Uncle Alf.

Uncle was a Cobbler and had his shop kitted out in the front room and sometimes he would allow me to stand behind the counter and take the money from the customers. I felt quite grown-up then, but I would only be about 10.

We would visit Mam's cousin Edie and Bill further down the road; her daughter, Eileen, played the piano beautifully. She had gained her cap and gown and my Dad loved to hear her play 'Dream of Olwen' and it still brings a tear in my eye whenever I hear it.

So many emotions and memories!

Christmas with The Daultons

Our Dining Room had a table in the middle of the floor with four chairs and two easy chairs, Lino as flooring and a snip rug which we all helped to make, out of rag pieces. Most of the time our Front Room was empty; except when Grandma Daulton came to live with us.

She brought with her a piano and I do know we had wonderful Christmases as Dad was a good pianist. The whole family would gather around the piano as Dad would play our favourites and we'd have a sing-a-long.

Grandma was very fond of the piano and insisted it was looked after.

I especially remember Dad playing these songs:

'One finger, one thumb – keep moving.'

'You are my sunshine'

'Oh! Susanna'

'This Old Man'

'Flight of the Bumblebee'

~

When it was time to make Christmas pudding, we all had to have a stir and Mam used to say, "make a wish!" and when the basin was empty, we all used to take turns to scrape the bowl and lick the spoon. We would all say, "My turn! My turn! Don't eat it all!" and "Mam, it's not fair, Gordon's had too much!"

Then Mam would say, "That's enough then, give it to me," and that would be the end of that.

Christmas Eve

I believed in Father Christmas right up to being 8 ½ years old. That year Gordon crept into the bedroom on Christmas Eve and whispered, "Are you awake, you lass?"

I said, "Go Away! Father Christmas won't come if we're awake!" But Gordon didn't seem worried.

"There isn't one." He said.

"Wh- Well where do we get our presents from then?"

"Dad brings 'em up."

I was so befuddled, I couldn't sleep and then I heard the stairs creek… and who should come in the bedroom? My Dad with the desk!

I couldn't believe it! I pretended I was asleep. I could see Dad from the landing light. All my dreams were shattered.

I heard Dad go back downstairs, so I risked a glance and saw the most amazing desk and stool. I couldn't resist a peep! It smelt so fresh of red paint and the newness of the wood inside. A wonderful surprise which I loved and treasured for many years.

Dolly Pegs

We used to sit at the table at home, preparing our Christmas decorations. Coloured paper chains were popular in those days and Mam would make clothes for a Peg Doll (Dolly pegs) for the top of the Christmas tree.

Afterwards, I had the dolly peg to play with and it would be redressed for next year. Crinkle Crepe paper was used to make a full skirt, strands of wool for her hair and a nice bow to rest on her head, not forgetting pipe cleaners for her arms, with bell-shaped sleeves covering her little body.

June's Dolly Peg

Christmas presents in them days weren't very plentiful, but our bellies were always full.

Magic painting books were popular, and we would always get an apple, an orange and a few sweets. One Christmas, my Dad brought home a big box and we were all so excited.

"What have you got Dad?"

He had that cheeky grin on his face which he only ever had when he had 'something up his sleeve' (as Mam would say). When he unwrapped it – what excitement!

It was a Hornby train with a full track. Oh! We absolutely loved it. Mind you, I didn't get much of a look in, with three brothers! I was a good sister and enjoyed watching them all have fun. I remember the boys also having a Meccano Set.

~

Winter was always a fun time because we did have lots of snow and frosts and had great time making slides on the road and plenty of snowballing. Of course, we could do that in those days as there wasn't the traffic about in the forties.

We would have hot aches in our hands when we went back in the house, but it was worth it. Gordon would nearly always manage to put some snow down my neck and he would eat the snow. Mam always said that's how Gordon ended up with Diphtheria.

Isolation

When Gordon caught Diphtheria, at 10 years old, he was laid on the couch waiting for the doctor to call, and I was sitting there offering him dolly mixtures until Mam came in from the kitchen and took them off me saying, "You'll choke him, you silly girl." I was only 6.

When the doctor arrived we all had to have a swab taken from our throat by a wooden spatula and it was horrible. It made me feel sick!

Gordon was taken to the isolation hospital at Scartho and stayed there for 4 weeks or more. The house was sealed up for a few days and we had to stay at Grandma's.

He was laid flat and the bed was tipped so his legs where higher than his head, so to help stop the infection spreading (from what I understand). Mam and Dad were allowed to see him, but we could only peep through the window. They had to wear special clothing.

When Gordon came home he used to shuffle around the house until he was strong again. I remember feeling very sad seeing him like that and it was great when he was back to his usual self, causing mischief.

Bare Necessities

During the forties, when money was tight, neighbours could rely on each other for helping with necessities. They would knock on the wall to draw your attention. "Have you a cup of sugar I could borrow? Or perhaps a couple of slices of bread?" In our case, we would need half a loaf!

I remember Mam, Gordon and myself going quite regularly to a lady's house in Durban Road called Wilomena and we used to really look forward to visiting because she always gave us a cup of Oxo with a slice of bread and we just loved it. She was such a cuddly, kindly lady.

Home Remedies

When I had whooping cough, Mam used to take me down to the gas house subway and the smell would get me coughing which helped break the congestion. I used to hate that as Mam used to tell me to put my finger down my throat to make myself sick. It sometimes worked.

I used to get tonsillitis quite a lot during the Winter months and I loved it when Mam would light a fire in the front bedroom because it was so cosy. When we had a cough Mam used to mix together lemon, vinegar, sugar and honey. However that would have been after the war.

Blitz & Sirens

The second World War started when I was only 2 years old. It ended after my 8th birthday.

It must have been very difficult for my Mam at that time, Bill was a big help to her. He would've been 11 years old when the war started. I was so young and did not understand the seriousness of it all, it seemed like a game to me.

The sirens would go off in the middle of the night and Mam would try and wake us all up. Difficult – when one of us woke up, another would go back to sleep!

She did try and find a routine. Once we were all up, we'd stand at the door with blankets around us or some sort of covering, waiting to go to the shelter. One at a time, she'd say, "Bill! Off you go... All clear. Off you go Derrick, with Gordon." Then she would run to the shelter with me.

On some occasions, we wouldn't have time to get into the shelter; so we would all huddle together in the under-the-stairs cupboard until the 'all clear' siren sounded.

Once, when Mam was giving me a strip wash in the bowl in front of the fire (I guess I would be about four years old) someone knocked on the door and in the next minute the siren sounded. I certainly got out quicker than I went in and for that air raid we didn't have time to get to the shelter. So, it was under the stairs we go…

Taking his Chances

Neighbours were very helpful during the war. There was a family that lived down Convamore Road and their back gate was opposite ours. Edgar, the eldest, very often used to check on the neighbours when we were all in the air raid shelters. We could hear his voice down the passageway; "Are you alright Mrs Daulton?" and "Are you alright Mrs Aisthorpe?" and so on… He would come into the garden on occasions, just to make sure. I expect it was quite reassuring for mothers that were on their own with children.

The man next door, Len, never did go into the shelter. He just stayed in his bed. Later on in life, Mam used to say, 'He took his chances…'

Dolly in the Debris

One day, I was staying with my Grandma and Dad came to pick me up to take me home. He was home on leave. Suddenly, the sirens sounded! We got to Welholme Road and saw that the aeroplanes were coming very low overhead, Dad shouted for me to get to the ground!

Thinking back, I can't remember being frightened, I suppose it was just something we'd become used to. Or, I was just too young to fully understand. I do remember Gordon screaming in the air raid shelter when the aeroplanes came over...

The air raid shelter had four bunk beds, in case we had to stay inside for a long time. When Grimsby got hit very badly, the air raid shelter door was blasted out. Afterwards, when the air raid had ended, we went back into the house and found the front window was shattered.

The next day, we walked over to see how my Auntie Lizzie was. There were no phones in those days! She lived almost opposite All Saints Church, on the corner of Catherine Street and Heneage Road. Luckily my Auntie was alright, but her windows were blasted out too.

As we were leaving my Auntie's house, we could see all the damage from the air strike; others had not been so lucky. I remember how sad I felt seeing a rag doll laying in a garden amongst all the debris. I don't know what had happened to that family.

Family Time

We all had a lot of fun and happy times with our cousins; Joan, Alan and John.

Their Dad, Uncle George, travelled quite a bit for his work. At one time, he worked on the ferries across from New Holland to Spurn Light House as a Steward. We loved going on the ferry when Uncle was working. I suppose we felt a sense of pride. At the time, I think we thought he owned it!

Afterwards he became a manager at Keelby 'Bricklayers Arms Pub'. We would go and stay for the weekend and had great times.

There was an apple tree outside the bedroom window which was against the wall – so it was easy to lean out of the window and pick the apples to munch in bed. A midnight snack!

We used to have a torch between us, so we could have it on, under the bed covers, as we weren't allowed to leave the light on because of the cost. We slept 3 at the bottom and 2 at the top.

My two older brothers were in a different bedroom, they didn't join in the fun.

Crisps and lemonade were a treat. I suppose we were spoilt on those occasions – or perhaps it was a bribe to keep us out of mischief?

On weekends, sometimes we would go to Keelby for the evening and come back to Grimsby after the pub had closed. That was fun too. During those times, there would be Aunt Alice and Uncle Horace, along with their two friends and Mam and Dad, the three boys and myself. We used to have a sing-a-long on the way home, songs such as:

It's a Sin to Tell a Lie
Kiss Me Good Night, Sergeant Major
It's a Long Way to Tipperary
Wish Me Luck (as You Wave Me Goodbye)

After a while Uncle moved to Louth, managing The King's Head Hotel; their house was at the back, down a yard. We'd have lots of fun there; but only for a very short time as Uncle then moved to Scunthorpe to manage the Conservative Club, (again only for a short time).

Now, that was a spooky place! We were sure it was haunted and of course, our imagination very often got the better of us. We used to frighten ourselves when we went to bed! We slept in the back bedroom and thought we heard noises. And of course, Gordon used to tell ghost stories and frighten us all to death (including himself) and there was one poem he used to recite to scare us, and it worked!

"*The night was creeping on the ground;*
She crept and did not make a sound
Until she reached the tree, and then
She covered it, and sole again
Along the grass beside the wall.

I heard the rustle of her shawl
As she threw blackness everywhere
Upon the sky and ground and air,
And in the room where I was hid:
But no matter what she did
To everything that was without,
She could not put my candle out.

So I stared at the night, and she
Stared back solemnly at me."

By James Brunton Stephens

Joan

Joan was a character and very special to me. We were very close growing up and were very much like my Mam and her Mum; we seemed to have the giggles just like they did. We always managed to bring out each other's cheeky side.

During the time my Auntie Elsie and Uncle George lived in Louth, Joan used to play the piano and I would sing along.

Her favourite song was Eileen Barton's 'If I Knew You Were Comin' (I'd 've Baked a Cake)...

"Well, well, well, look who's here.
I haven't seen you in many a year.
If I knew you were comin' I'd 've baked a cake,
baked a cake, baked a cake.
If I knew you were comin' I'd 've baked a cake.
How-ja do. How-ja do, How-ja do..."

Songwriters: Al Hoffman / Bob Merrill / Clem Watts
If I Knew You Were Comin' (I'd 've Baked a Cake) lyrics ©
Warner/Chappell Music, Inc, Music & Media Int'l, Inc

Joan did not mince her words; if she didn't like things (whatever they were) she would say so.

Perhaps she might say, "I don't like your hair done like that – reminds me of that film star with her short, cropped hair," or "Why don't you have a perm?" or "Are you alright duck? You don't look very well."

When she was small, Joan loved to drink vinegar. I don't know how often but whenever we were in her company she would have a guzzle. Mam always used to say to her "It'll dry your blood up!"

The Long Walk

One day, I went to Louth with Mam to visit Auntie and Uncle. Joan and I took it upon ourselves to go to Cadwell Races. I was about 14 at the time and Joan was 17; it was a very hot day and we set off walking. We were rather naive and didn't realise how far we had to walk!

We hadn't been gone long when we decided to stop at a very old-looking cottage to ask for a drink of water. We hadn't even considered that we would get thirsty.

"Are you going to knock on the door and ask?" said Joan.

Joan stood behind me as I knocked on the door.

Oh my goodness! From nowhere, came this gander!

We soon turned heel and managed to get safely to the other side of the gate.

A lady eventually came outside after hearing all the commotion. She kindly gave us a glass of water. We told her where we were going and a look of amusement passed across her face, but she didn't comment.

We soon had second thoughts and decided to go back to Louth.

It was a good job we did! We learnt afterwards it would have been much too far – and really, I don't think we had a clue.

Looking back now, Mam and Auntie Elsie weren't at all pleased when they found out about our adventure.

~

Joan and I had always spoken on the phone; we always ended up having a good laugh, even if we were only laughing at ourselves. We'd have a giggle over nothing…

Our aches and pains would come into conversation and we used to say, "We get more and more like our mothers every day."

I do miss our dear chats and laughter.

Giggling Aunts

Auntie Elsie and Mam got on very well. We called them 'The Giggling Aunts' because they always found something to laugh about; even if it was something silly they had done. They could always see the funny side of things.

Uncle George used to say; "You silly pair of buggers!"

In later years, Mam went away on holiday with them. They had some good laughs.

The Giggling Aunts, Uncle George & Kit – holidaying together

Poor Uncle George! Although deep down, I bet he enjoyed being with them. He was a bit of a ladies' man and they used to have a giggle and take the mickey as Uncle would wear a night cap on his head when he went to bed because his head used to get cold.

I remember, vividly, a time when Auntie Elsie was staying at our house and Mam had been telling her about the rent collector and that he was due that day. So Mam said, "Elsie, when the rent man calls this morning, you'll have to go in the kitchen otherwise you'll start me off laughing."

The rent man always caused fits of giggles because of his quirky mannerisms and the way he spoke.

Anyway, when he arrived, Auntie Elsie hid away in the kitchen and Mam invited him in. Mam still had difficulty keeping a straight face because she knew that Auntie Elsie would be behind the door, giggling.

When the rent man left, Mam opened the door to Auntie Elsie laughing so loudly. Their laughter was infectious.

Auntie Lizzie

After the war, Auntie Lizzie, Mam's eldest sister, moved from Heneage Road to Peaks Field Avenue. She was a lovely, fussy lady who liked lots of fun. She always styled her hair in a bun and I can't remember her ever not wearing a pinafore.

Whenever we went to visit Auntie Lizzie she always offered us a sweet out of her wooden biscuit barrel. Always the same sweets; 'Nuttall's Mintoes'. I think we felt privileged as we didn't get to use much of our sweet ration.

Auntie Lizzie never seemed to use her front room. But it was nicely furnished with a Moquette three-piece suite and in her window, she had a big Aspidistra plant in a pot on a tall wooden stand.

It was a very sad time when she passed away. She had been ill for a long time and I remember being with Mam on many occasions when she cared for her. I learnt later that she had breast cancer.

Her husband, Uncle Ted, was killed in France during the war. His twin brother, Jack, lived with Auntie Lizzie until she passed.

And then Jack came to live with us.

Jack

Jack was a very slender man, who dressed very smart, used a walking stick and always wore a trilby hat, which most men did, in those days.

He slept in the spare bed in the back bedroom, with my three brothers. They used to take the mickey and have lots of fun.

I remember him being a nice, friendly man and he used to tell my brothers little stories and ditties in bed…

"Wherever you may be, let the wind go free — it was the wind that killeth me."

"A fart is a very peculiar thing,
It gives the body ease
It warms the bed on a winter's night
And gives music to the flees."

I remember Jack leaving our home after a while to go and live in the country. He did come back and visit us a couple of times.

Godparents

Uncle Sam & Aunt Holly's Wedding Day

I have some lovely memories of Uncle Sam and Aunt Holly. We had many great Afternoon Teas and evening sing-songs with them after the war.

Aunt Holly used to make yummy tasting cakes and always made a lovely spread of food. Her father was a Master Baker, so I expect she learnt from him.

When I was about 18, I made a Madeira cake and took it round because I felt very proud of how lovely it looked, and to get her approval. But unfortunately, she detected what I hadn't done… She said, "You haven't made this with butter, have you?"

I said, "No margarine…"

"Never shortcut your baking June, Madeira cake needs to be made with butter!" Mind you, she did say it was very nice.

So that was a lesson learnt.

Aunt Alice
& Uncle Horace

I did stay with Aunt Alice and Uncle Horace, my Mam's brother, for a short time in Peterborough; they lived in a Caravan at that time – a lovely residential site in Werrington. They were so kind to me and we had some great laughs together.

My Mam and the family were also considering moving and living in Peterborough.

I got myself a good job working at the British Horticulture company in Walton, as a Filing Clerk for which I loved. But I was only there for 6 months as the family decided not to move, which was disappointing as Mam was looking forward to moving to Peterborough. So I decided to go back home. I had even found a place for us to live, but it wasn't meant to be.

~

We would go to the cinema once a week – 'Cowboy Adventures' Aunt Alice loved them!

There was no television and we always listened to the radio, we especially enjoyed 'The Man in Black' a spooky, Paul Temple crime drama.

Later in life, when Ray and I moved to Peterborough and again when Julie was born – we visited Aunt Alice and Uncle Horace regularly. We then lived in a Caravan and they had moved into a house.

Aunt Alice would sometimes look after Julie and have her for a few hours… Julie remembers her saying, "Remember when you need to go to the toilet, you mustn't say *poo* – you say, I want to do my business."

Margaret (my friend who used to live opposite us in the caravan) loved visiting Aunt Alice because we usually ended up in a fit of giggles over her expressions and things she would say!

She was lovely.

Aunt and Uncle decided to retire and move back to Grimsby.

In later years I looked after her often and unfortunately she developed dementia. She always recognised Ray's voice and the grandchildren loved to visit her.

Aunt Alice and the Grandchildren celebrating her 90th Birthday

Aunt May, Uncle Alf & Doris

When I was 8 or 9, I would have holidays in Boston, just after the war, and stay with Aunt May, Uncle Alf and Cousin Doris. I'd travel on my own after Mam put me on the train.

Uncle Alf, Aunt May & Cousin Doris

I was taken care of by the guardsman in the Guard's Van. There I would sit on a box or trunk. I was very quiet, didn't utter a word, unless I was spoken to. I wasn't afraid, I just felt wonderfully grown-up. In those days, children were told to 'speak when you are spoken to.' In other words, don't speak out of turn and remember your please and thank you's and 'children should be seen and not heard.'

Not that we weren't allowed to be children (far from it) but we were always kept in our place.

The Boston trips were lovely holidays and I was terribly spoilt in the nicest way. Aunt May loved me to wash her hair. I would stand on a stool over the deep, white kitchen sink and with the lifebuoy soap; wash her hair, just thinking about it I can smell it as if I was there.

The kitchen was quite a large one and it had a big walk in larder, full of bottled fruits and big aluminium containers of flour on the floor and dishes for the two lovely cats (they were fed raw eggs every day).

After I had washed Aunt May's hair, I had to do my party piece in the corner of the kitchen; I use to go tap dancing, so Aunt May always insisted that I did some tap dancing and acrobats. She'd then allow me to push her waves in. Thinking back, Aunt May had a lovely head of hair, deep natural waves.

My Uncle Alf would perhaps sometimes come into the kitchen and have one or two words, but I didn't see very much of him; only at meal times, as he spent long hours in his work room, Tailoring. Both Aunt and Uncle were Tailor and Tailoress. I very often used to see Uncle from his work room window overlooking the beautifully kept garden.

There would be two deck chairs, one for my Aunt and one for myself; she would sometimes come and sit a while when she had done her work.

One particular time, I remember sauntering through the lawn looking at the fruit trees and I gently touched a young apple and it fell into my palm, *'Oh dear,'* I thought, not daring to look up to the window, where Uncle would sit at his work.

'What shall I do?' and without any delay, I placed it on the ground, praying that the incident had never happened as Uncle loved his garden. He also tended an allotment at the bottom of the garden.

The house was very large, but the rooms were very seldom used, only at weekends. All the windows had sun canopies and the stairs were very wide. At the top of the stairs, there was a large, wide stained-glass window. Funnily enough, I never liked that window; I used to rush past it.

The landing served four bedrooms and a bathroom/toilet. The small room being Uncle's work room, which I never peeped in. I slept in another small room. Then there were two double bedrooms facing the front of the house.

My cousin, Doris, who was 9 years older than me, would take me on walks with their dog; a spaniel called Monty. He was a lovely dog but the only time he was allowed in the house was in the evening and he had a bed in the wash house, which was in the house adjacent to the kitchen and it also accommodated a toilet, which nowadays the wash house is called a Utility Room. I loved the smell of the toilet paper. We weren't used to so much luxury!

In the day time, Monty would very often lay in the shed where he had another bed, but he did have the run of the garden.

Doris would also take me into town when she wasn't working. She worked in Boston Town as a Pharmacy Assistant. We also used to go and visit a dear old lady that lived across the road in The Almshouses, these were provided for the poor or infirm. But later were used (I believe) as rented accommodation, they were very cosy and small. The lady we visited seemed very old, wore long black clothing and had difficulty in getting about. Doris would do her shopping for her. I remember the lady taking my hand so gently and giving me a lovely smile when Doris introduced me to her as her little cousin from Grimsby.

There were also twin girls and a family we used to visit, further down the road. I cannot remember their names, but they always made a fuss of me, asking me lots of questions about my tap dancing and I would do a little routine.

I remember going on the stage at the Palace Theatre, in Grimsby; tapdancing and singing with a partner.

> *"Snap your tie on and click your hair*
> *We've gotta get going to the country fayre*
> *Fetch the buggie and hitch the mare*
> *We've gotta get going to the country fayre*
> *Big tops and side shows*
> *Just take your pick*
> *We stop for popcorns*
> *But I want a toffee apple on a stick*
> *So, spend your money and see the sights*
> *We aint-a-gonna leave until they douse the lights*
> *And when it's over – remember this!*
> *We cuddle up a little bit and steal a kiss*
> *Go on an spoon*
> *The harvest moon won't care*
> *It's so much nicer – than going to the county fayre."*

~

Remembering Boston, when Doris got married in 1947; I was one of the bridesmaids and my cousin Joan from Scunthorpe was another. There were 5 bridesmaids altogether. Anyway, our dresses were in beautiful powder blue crepe; and Uncle Alf and Aunt May made them.

The wedding was a grand affair and I remember as I walked into the church Botolphs, Boston Stump it looked so magnificent and beautiful and I felt such a feeling of pride and excitement and what a wonderful day!

After the evening do, I remember us staying in a big house, but not Aunt May's. I believe it was Aunt May's sister, Mrs Whyers; she used to have a florist shop in Boston. She was a very colourful lady, some would say perhaps a little eccentrically dressed. But she was a very nice, friendly lady. Sleeping there was great for us children, sleeping on the floor with nice fluffy blankets and rather posh to what we were used to.

Norman & Doris' Wedding, 1947

My Dad was the Best Man to Norman the Bridegroom. He was a tall handsome chap from Grimsby and was introduced to Doris through my Dad.

Unfortunately, the marriage wasn't to last and Doris later remarried to Alan.

During the time Ray and I lived in Peterborough, we visited Boston on many occasions, when Julie was a baby. They absolutely adored her.

We had many an enjoyable times with them as they belonged to the Veteran club and went on cycle rides. We continued to do so when we first came back to Grimsby, for many years.

Our Godson, Russell, then only about 4, would come with us to Boston and he absolutely loved it. He rode a small tricycle and Doris and Alan made such a fuss of him.

We are lucky to have so many nice memories to treasure over the years.

Treasured Friends

We lived in a very big community where friends were family and we all played together, most of the time.

Eileen

Eileen and I became new friends after both of our Dads passed away. She told me, "My Daddy's just died as well, would you like to be my friend?"

Her name was Eileen Coulam and we are still good friends. She is now known as Eileen

Veermersch. We lost touch when I moved to Birmingham in 1957 but when we came to live in Grimsby in 1979, we continued our friendship.

We were pupils of a class of 48. At an impressionable and tender age of 11, up until this time, we only knew each other vaguely to say hello and perhaps have the occasional game in the playground then suddenly within such a short time, we almost became inseparable.

I remember Eileen was sweet on a boy at school once... called John. He didn't go to Welholme school, he belonged to the private school; St James. She wanted to know 'a song about Johnny', so my Mam wrote the words out for her and we have often laughed about it since.

> *"Oh Johnny! Oh Johnny, how you can love.*
> *Oh Johnny! Oh Johnny, heavens above*
> *You make my sad heart jump with joy*
> *And when I'm near you*
> *I just can't sit still a minute*
> *And its oh! Johnny oh! Johnny*
> *Please tell me dear*
> *What makes me love you so*
> *You're not handsome it true*
> *But when I look at you*
> *It's just! Oh! Johnny oh! Johnny oh!"*

Two Friends on an Adventure

Eileen had a dear Aunt and Uncle who lived in the country of Wickenby and it was suggested that Eileen and I should take a short holiday with them. I was a puny, little thing and could do with fattening up. Our two mums decided it would be good for both of us, to get some nice fresh, country air. We were so excited!

We were allowed to travel alone on the train, I absolutely loved trains and thought of them very fondly. When the day came for us to travel our two Mams took us to the station. As the train arrived on the platform, we were so excited, and I am sure rather apprehensive; I know I was, especially going somewhere strange.

We were given strict instructions to be very good and to look out for Aunty who would be waiting for us. We each had our own seat on either side of the window.

In those days, there were separate carriages that accommodated about 8 people; two long seats facing each other. Our legs were swinging with excitement as the train made its way through the countryside. The train was almost empty with just a few locals going a little further along the track. So, we had the carriage to ourselves. As the train pulled into the station, there was Eileen's Aunty, waiting. A rather plump lady, with short cropped straight hair but she had such a pleasant smile and a rosy complexion, just as you would expect to see from someone living in the country.

The weather was glorious, and the sun beamed down upon us and kissed our cheeks as we stepped out onto the platform. We passed our cases to Aunty and she hugged and kissed us. I already felt like part of the family! The station was very pretty with an array of flower beds. Aunty said we had only a short walk to the farm; some 20 minutes down the lane. As we walked, she asked us about the train journey and hoped we would enjoy our stay. She also said we would have a friend to play with occasionally, who lived further down the lane. When we finally arrived at the house, we were both feeling rather tired; I think the excitement and train journey had worn us out.

The house stood on its own with a pan tiled roof, and a lovely garden with a couple of fruit trees, flower beds and on one side, there was a vegetable patch. Approaching the back door, I noticed how small and heavy it looked. And as Aunty went to open it, the sneck on it sounded so sharp and hard; this door led straight into the kitchen and the smell of the dinner was so appetising, my tummy stated to rumble.

"Come along children, I'll show you were your bedroom is." Aunty said.

We followed her through the kitchen and into the living room; there stood a round table covered with a chenille cloth and on it a rather large oil lamp. The fireplace was big and open with shiny brass slipper boxes on either side and a companion set; the latter was used for picking up coal out of the coal box to put on the fire. The coal box stood against one of the slipper boxes. A snip rug was placed in the front of the hearth. Snip rugs were made out of strips of material usually the back was made of sacking or hessian and the implement that was used to pull the strips of material through was like a big crochet hook with a bone handle. There were four kitchen chairs placed around the table and a big rocking chair sat near the window facing the fire. The stairs were behind a door adjacent to the living room – it was rather a dark, dismal stairway that was very narrow, steep and winding. So, unlike a town house we had both left. Immediately at the top of the stairs were 3 doors with the landing just big enough to stand on.

Aunty opened the second bedroom door and said, "Here we are, this is your room. Unpack your suitcases – I have emptied a draw each for you." Pointing to a rather shabby chest of draws.

"When you've finished, dinner will be ready. I expect you are hungry little girls, aren't you?"

"Yes!" We both replied, and we quickly started to unpack our cases. When we had finished unpacking, we went downstairs, and Aunty said to us, "Would you like a drink before we have dinner?"

We both enjoyed a glass of lemonade. It was harvesting time and Eileen's Uncle Charlie was out in the fields so when the meal was ready, Aunty Edie asked Eileen to call him in for dinner.

We both trotted off down the road to find him. In no time at all, we were back in the house, Uncle Charlie was in the kitchen washing his hands and then came in to living room to say hello. I thought he was a lovely, friendly gentleman and took to him straight away. On one occasion, Eileen and myself took Uncle Charlie's dinner to him and a bottle of cold tea. I wasn't very impressed with the cold tea – yuck! But now in my senior years, I very often drink cold tea as I sit and hold my cup for ages.

Aunty Edie would do her shopping in Market Rasen and one day, she decided to take us to the cinema. We really enjoyed that day out and noticed how friendly everyone was to each other. I suppose it was because it was such a small community, and everyone knew each other well.

The girl that lived further down the lane was called Daphne. She lived in a thatched cottage and Eileen and I enjoyed her company and had lots of fun, along the beck. They also had plenty of apples to eat and we'd naughtily take them upstairs to eat in bed. The core was put under the bed and I expect Aunty wouldn't be very pleased when she saw them, but nothing was ever said.

Uncle Charlie and Aunty Edie had two sons; the eldest, Norman and his young lady, Irene, used to invite us to join them on a walk down the lane with Bruce, the dog.

The stray cow used to come into the garden from the fields at the back of the house. I didn't like that very much, I was a bit scared. They had a pretty garden and Aunty asked us to pick some sweet peas to bring into the house and the perfume was wonderful, they gave a lovely aroma to the living room. There were lots of 'Daddy long legs' and moths. They used to hover around the oil lamp at night. It made me shudder; I didn't like moths.

The toilet was outside, with two seats in it made of wood. So, at night we would use the pot under the bed.

When the holiday was over, Aunty took us to the station and made sure we were safely on the train. She gave us a big hug and wished us a safe journey home. When we arrived back in Grimsby, both our mums were there to welcome us. What a happy holiday that was and it led onto lots more times together.

We were together on holiday when I met Ray, my husband to be, when I was 16 at Peterborough.

Bubsey

Barbara Horsewood (Bubsey) came from a large family but their house was immaculate; nothing posh, but her Mam worked her fingers to the bone.

Remembering in those days, wash days took all day. Their house was bigger than ours, they had an extra building which was the wash house with a big mangle, big wooden rollers, wash boiler which was stoked up underneath to get the water hot, a dolly tub and Dolly Pegs or posher, rinsing was often done outside under the cold-water tap.

Bubsey used to show off; sometimes we used to encourage her. She would get a full bottle of cod liver oil and drink it in front of us and of course, we used to say, "Awe Bubsey, how could you?!"

And then she would bring it all back up in the outside sink and we'd laugh ourselves silly.

When Bubsey ever came to my house to call for me, she never knocked on the door. She just shouted through the letterbox… "June!"

One time when she shouted me, and my Uncle who lived further up in Welholme Road was at our house and thought it so funny, he couldn't get over it. As the years rolled by it would come up in conversation.

Bubsey, was a character. If she was so minded she would come up and push you into the hedge! I've seen her many a time in later life and we've laughed about everything we used to get up to!

Barbara & June

Baby Minding

I used to love baby minding. In fact it was quite popular after the war, as there were lots of babies and small children in the neighbourhood.

I just had to knock at the neighbour's door who you knew had a baby and say, "May I take your baby out please?" More often than not, the answer would be yes.

One family in particular I used to babysit for, lived in Torrington Street. The baby would sit in a beautiful, high coach-built pram. I was very responsible. We would walk to People's Park sit and watch the ducks in the pond for a while and then I would take the baby home. She nearly always slept through. It gave her Mother a chance to get some work done. (Mind you, having said that I would never have allowed anyone to take my babies out when I became a mother!)

When Barbara, who lived next door to us on Welholme Road, gave birth to Paul I looked after him a lot too; fed him, changed him and took him out most days.

He was a lovely little boy. I made some blue flannelette pyjamas for baby Paul whilst I was at school. Eileen made her own set for one of the babies she minded. I don't think my machining was very perfect; however they fitted him quite well.

Monkey Parading

Eileen and I had great times together in our early teens going cadetting when we were about 14. The cadets used to come and stay at the Weelsby Camp, which is now the park. Mam used to call it 'monkey parading', walking along the prom at Cleethorpes hoping to get talking to boys.

I remember one boy in particular, Raymond Prince, he came from Darlington. It was all innocent good fun.

We used to walk to the prom then to wonderland, where there were a few rides, side stalls and the skating rink and a big dipper. Sometimes we'd go to the boating lake and perhaps have a few chips and then walk all the way home again. We never thought anything about the long walks in those days.

Mind you, sometimes our shoes would come off, whether it was cold or not. Mam used to say, "You'll know all about it my girl, when you get older."

When I went dancing in stilettos, just the same walk home, I'd carry them in my hands; as a great many more of the girls would do the same.

Fun With Friends

Around the age of 14, there were workmen down Welholme Road, digging trenches. I was with my friends and I suppose we were being a bit flirty and silly. After a while, we got to know some of the workers; one chap was called Stan and we used to greet him with, "Now then Stan, you dirty, old man!" Another was named Joe, we used to get his attention and say, "Hello Joe! What do you know?" He always replied, "I know nothing," with a cheeky grin on his face.

It was all good fun, with friends, no offence taken. We had some good times.

~

When I was 16, Mam, Eileen and I went to Scunthorpe to stay with Auntie Elsie for the weekend and I had just recently been in hospital to have my appendix out.

In the evening, Eileen and I decided to go to the pictures in Scunthorpe and my Auntie lived on the Queensway which was about 3 miles from the town centre. We got the bus and off we trotted, Mam and Auntie saying, "Be careful and come straight back, no hanging about and make sure you get on the right bus."

The eventuality happened; we caught the bus okay but got off at the wrong stop! And we ended up having to walk about 1 and ½ miles. When we arrived home Mam and Auntie were worried sick.

~

Eileen, Pauline Wright and I had many a great times, especially Saturday nights when the RAF Boys came in from Binbrook and Manby. They were very casual acquaintances but lovely dancers. A lot of RAF Boys used to frequent the Alex Dance Hall in Top Town, but I wasn't allowed to go there and the RAF Camps and Pubs were a definite 'No-No'.

Barbara, Pauline & June

Pauline, June & Eileen – 'monkey parading'

One evening, I remember coming home from the Gaiety Dance Hall with my dancing shoes in my hand. I'd be about 17 at the time, and there was a night watchman in his hut with a lovely roaring coke fire so I stood talking to him for about 10 minutes.

We chatted about the cold evening and how lovely it was to see and feel the warmth of the fire. I remember him asking why I wasn't wearing my shoes and I said;

"Because my feet are killing me due to all the dancing!" He just laughed.

~

115

The first bike I bought was a second hand one, which I bought off Eileen. It cost £5 and it was what we called a sit-up-and-beg type. It served me well for a couple of years, then I bought myself a Raleigh racing bike with derailleur gears. I loved it!

I often went cycling; the furthest I went was to Louth. Bill was also a keen cyclist. He belonged to the cycle club in Hainton square and went all over. I remember him especially going to Lake Windemere, Mam was quite worried about him, as it seemed to be such a long way those days.

One day, I had been out on my bike to Cleethorpes and just arrived home. Bearing in mind, I had recently bought a pair of trousers with dogtooth check; very smart. Anyway, my Aunt Holly came to visit and the first thing she said to me was, "June, I don't like to see you in those trousers, they aren't for girls."

So, I said, "But Aunty! It's better than showing all I've got! Wearing a dress for cycling!"

Anyway, she understood and said, "Oh! Perhaps not but don't wear them too often, will you?" I gladly agreed.

Cinema on Sundays

In my teen years during the winter, on Sunday evenings, Eileen, Pauleen and I went to the pictures. Usually, we went to the Queen's Picture House down Alexandra Road, Grimsby. Then on the way home, we'd call in the snack bar for a warm drink, although Mam always had a warm drink waiting for me.

It was a ritual in our house. Mam would always lay the table ready for breakfast but would leave on the corner of the table a biscuit or sandwich and a cup with cocoa ready to put the hot water in, which was keeping hot on the side oven fireplace.

The front door was always locked but the key was hanging on a string on the inside of the door which you would put your hand in the letterbox and pull it through; it was quite common to do in those days. There was very little crime. People would never think to lock their doors if they were just going up the road shopping. Thinking back, we were open to crime. Especially, leaving the key hanging! Mam would be in bed when we came home late from dancing. Although I don't think she ever slept until we came in, she would always shout, "Is that you, June?" Or Derrick, Gordon, Bill...Mind you, I don't know what she would have done if a strange voice answered!

~

Once when I came home from the Gaiety I unlocked the door and walked in; my gosh! I was petrified! Hanging in the hall, was a hung chicken with its feathers still on! My Mam wondered what on earth was wrong; hearing me scream frightened her to death too. Bill had come in before me and knowing I would be scared, thought he would play a trick on me. Mam was very cross with him! And told him to take it in the kitchen and hang it on the coal house door, which he did. He did say he was sorry afterwards, but he said it with a grin, so I don't think he was.

There was a special time with Bill when he had been in Egypt for a year; he came home on leave and surprised me by coming to the Gaiety to meet me. I had no idea! I can still see in my mind's eye so vividly as I walked out of the door of the Gaiety, that familiar figure – tall and smart – still with his uniform on, Oh! I felt so proud! I was on cloud 9 walking home with him.

We seemed to sit talking for hours; he was there during the Suez crisis. I used to write to him quite often whilst he was away. He brought home a pair of beautiful stockings, made of silk, a pair each for Gwen (his young lady), Mam and me. You wouldn't dare to put them on your feet unless they were rolled up and wore cotton gloves to put them on in case you snag them. They seemed to last for ages; gently washing them after each time you wore them. They had nice shaped heels with a seam up the back. Sheer luxury!

Before he went to Egypt, Bill came home from the Gaiety one night and showed me how he learnt the Jitterbug. Well he got hold of me, and swung me through his legs, Mam shouted, "Be careful Bill, you'll hurt her! You're a bit near the sideboard." Anyway, I was alright and enjoyed it.

Unmentionables

I remember the day I bought my first bra; 32A and the cups were circular and stitched and padded, exquisite form.

I wore it for the first time at a dance. I danced with a boy, perhaps too close, and when I walked back to my seat, I noticed my bust shape was dented in! Yet another embarrassing situation! I had to press them and they popped out again.

I can laugh at the thought now but at the time, I hoped no one noticed.

One evening when I was dancing, my garter – which was popular to wear then… slipped down to my ankle. I soon whipped it off and fortunately I did have a suspender belt on! So, my stocking didn't fall down. Rather an embarrassing moment. But nothing was said by the boy I was dancing with, just an embarrassed smile between the two of us.

At fifteen years old, I was allowed to go The Gaiety Dance Hall. However, I do believe that if my Dad had been alive this wouldn't have been the case. The Gaiety Dance Hall was supposedly one of the best dance floors around. It was a sprung wooden floor and had alcoves all round with tables and chairs in and Passion Alley was popular at New Year – used for having a private kiss. This was a passage down the inside wall. All the big named bands came to the Gaiety. On a Thursday evening and cost 3^{s}6^d. Joe Loss, Edmundo Ross, Dr Crock and his Crackpots, Geraldo, Ted Heath, Victor Silvester, Eric Delany, Cyril Stapleton, Sid Lawrence and many more. We use to have great times, but alcohol wasn't allowed.

~

On special occasions, like Christmas or birthdays, Pauline and I would have a glass of port before we went out.

I used to go around to her house, but Mam never knew what I was up to. I know, naughty!

Sometimes, I would even borrow a pair of Pauline's drop earrings. Mam didn't like to see me in them though; she always said they looked common.

Pauline was never ready, she'd take forever, standing in front of the mirror putting her makeup on, patting her face with loose powder. There would be clouds of powder dust around her...

We'd have such a giggle about it.

They were the good times!

My Love, Ray

My teenage years, from 15, focused a lot around dancing, cycling and even going regularly to Beetle Drives, which were very popular in the 50's. In fact, I had quite a few prizes for my bottom drawer i.e. tea cloths, tumblers, dusters, dishcloths, odd pillow slips, salt/pepper pots, towels, anything in those days were gratefully received. Mam used to say, "What have you come home with this time?"

I was just 16 when I met Ray in Woolworths. I was on holiday in Peterborough at Aunt Alice and Uncle Horace's.

Ray was with two more friends, as they were stationed at RAF Langtoft and had decided to go into Peterborough, swimming, but had other thoughts. Ray has since told me, they were looking for a bit of 'Talent', our eyes met across the counter and our story begins…

I was with Eileen and Ray asked if we would like to go for coffee, so we said, "That would be very nice."

Mam and Aunt Alice were with us, but elsewhere in Woolworths, anyway I went over to them to get their approval and Mam said, "Yes but be careful. We will see you back at Auntie's."

That evening we went back into Peterborough and met them to go to the Pictures. It was the start of a beautiful romance.

Ray, aged 16, A Sea Cadet

I learnt that Ray was being posted abroad a few weeks later, so it meant letter-writing for 4 years and only seeing each other every 6 months.

During that time, Ray's Dad and I also often wrote to each other. He was a lovely man and very supportive.

Mine & Ray's parting stood the test of time and we were married 4 years later, to the day.

Sadly, his Dad passed away suddenly in March, prior to the wedding. So he wasn't there to see us married, but I am sure he was with us in spirit. He certainly would be very proud of his son now.

Our Wedding Day

Our marriage took place at All Saints Church on June 8th 1957. It was a very simple wedding with 20 guests and the reception was at The County Hotel, in Brighowgate.

Derrick paid for the wedding reception. We had a lovely meal which was ham salad, with trifle for dessert. The wedding cake was made by Miss Bee, Master Baker at the time. A friend from work, Eileen Russel, made my dress.

My bridesmaids were my niece Janet, and two friends, Janet and Sandra who I worked with.

The sun shone for a short time, so we managed to get some nice photos then the heavens opened with torrential rain and thunderstorms, but we managed to keep dry.

Having three loving brothers, I was spoilt for choice, so to save arguments I asked Uncle Horace to give me away. He honoured me by saying yes.

Dave Boyton was Ray's best man; he was stationed with Ray in Germany and became good friends, which still continues. Dave and Jo (his wife) live in Halesowen; they too have celebrated their Diamond Wedding Anniversary. We both have been truly blessed.

We didn't go on a honeymoon as money was scarce, we stayed at Mam's house and travelled to Birmingham after the weekend, ready for work. I managed to get a job within a week at Zip the Cleaners, sewing tags on garments, that lasted for a few months, then I worked at Antlers the Saddlers making leather satchels, briefcases and luggage. I used to cut the patterns from templates ready for the machines.

Another job I had, was checking "Peerage" Brassware to see if they were lacquered properly. Oh, I've certainly had varied work!

We started our life together in an Attic flat in Erdington, Birmingham. We hadn't been married many months when I found a lump in my breast. Anyway, my Mam came over and during that time stayed with Ray's Mam and all turned out okay; it was a fibro adenoma, which was removed.

During my single life, I was honoured to be a bridesmaid three times. So the superstition 'three times a bridesmaid, never a bride' went out the window straight away!

I was a bridesmaid first to my cousin Doris, second to Aunt Alice and third to my eldest brother, Bill.

Bill married Gwen in 1953. Gwen already had a young daughter, who was called Janet. Bill adopted her and raised her as his own.

The family of three were living with us in Welholme Road when Gwen gave birth to a baby girl. They named her Lynn. I was honoured to be present at her birth and heard her first cry. Lynn was a lovely, contented baby. I was only 18 years old at the time.

Sadly, 16 years, Gwen passed away. She was only 48 years old when she died.

A while later, Bill met Karen and remarried and together they had a daughter, named Sharon. My brother would have been very proud of her achievements in life.

Lynn & Bill

Mr & Mrs Herrick

Wedding presents

When Mam had to give her factory jobs up, she did domestic work at a house in Heneage Road, and they had two children. I used to look after them on the occasional evening. They were very nice people and when I got married I was given a set of saucepans and I had them for many years.

Those days you were very lucky to get expensive presents.

I remember our next-door neighbour, Mrs Aisthorpe buying me a chrome teapot and a tin opener which was very heavy and reminded me of a bull's head. Anyway, the first time I used it, it slipped, and I cut my middle finger. I've still got the scar to show for it!

Pillow slips, tea cloths and towels were popular presents, but I was fortunate enough to be given a candlewick bedspread from Aunt Holly and Uncle Sam.

Ray's family bought us a canteen of cutlery which had bone handles and EPNS, but they very soon became very tarnished over a few years. I still have a tablespoon left but it has lost all of its shine. I use it for measuring flour and sugar when I'm baking.

Ray's Jobs

Ray had various jobs, working at British United Trawlers on the docks and part time at Greenwoods outfitters and Cavendish Wood House Furnishings. Fortunately, one day he was talking to someone and they suggested he applied to Ciba Geigy – the chemical plant at Great Coates. They were setting people on; so he applied and got a job. This opportunity put us back on the 'right track' and we never looked back.

He had some good work mates and had many get-togethers over the years with a brilliant social life.

Getting Around

When we were in the Caravan we managed to afford ourselves a three-wheeler car Messerschmitt. We loved it, Julie and I used to sit in the back. I might add that I was very slim then...

We travelled to lots of places in that little car, once we travelled from Peterborough to Liverpool to attend a wedding.

~

Remembering my first encounter with a Lambretta scooter was in the year 1959. We lived at the school in Forster Street, Birmingham and Ray had just brought it home. It was our first form of transport before we changed it for a Messerschmitt. Ray reluctantly let me have a ride on it around the playground. I started it up okay and rode in little circles but when I stopped I forgot to take it out of gear, got off, and it went off on its own! Luckily, Ray caught it before it hit the wall. I hasten to add, I didn't drive it again!

We had some happy times out and about on the scooter, travelled to Grimsby from Birmingham in the winter; we'd got our leathers on, but it was so cold and when we arrived at Mam's, we were almost frozen to the bone. It took us ages to warm up! Mam was pleased to see us but not very impressed saying, "Fancy coming all this way in the cold?!"

Ray knitted me a lovely orange jumper in poodle wool and wore it on many occasions on the scooter during the summer months. I was so proud of it and it fitted perfectly. We often did knit together.

When Ray smashed his leg and was in hospital for a few weeks, he made Lisa's newborn twins a cardigan each. I did the sewing up and picked up the occasional stitch. Ha! Ha!

~

We then bought a 3-wheeler Reliant which we loved. This was after Lisa was born. It came to the time when we had to decide whether to keep it. The car needed quite a lot of work and we also needed a new inside toilet door, so we asked the children;

"Right girls, we can either have the car repaired or sell it and use the money for the toilet and a holiday?"

They cheered and decided on the holiday. The car was sold, and we paid £37.10 per adult for 10 days at the Lyons Mesana Hotel in Benidorm. What a wonderful holiday! We arrived early morning and when we opened the blinds as the sun came up it was a sight to behold, we were so happy, and the girls made new friends and the Spanish waiters made so much fuss of them.

~

After getting married and living in Birmingham, we moved to Peterborough. We lived there for 13 years and our children went to Fulbridge School along with their cousins; Steve, Bruce, Carl and Glenn.

Ray worked shifts at Perkins Diesel Engines and we bought a caravan and lived in that for three years.

We then moved into a council house at Dogsthorpe for 2 years and saved up to pay for a deposit for our private house which those days were £100 deposit and the house cost was £1,800 for a three-bedroom terrace property. We absolutely loved it and felt so proud we had saved our deposit. That was 2 months before Christmas and the bank book was empty!

I managed to get a job at the local pub on a Sunday morning, cleaning and I was allowed to take the children. Lisa was still in a push chair and Julie used to love it because she liked putting the beer mats on the tables. Anyway, it gave me spare cash to have a lovely Christmas without spending silly.

~

When we lived in the caravan, we had some very special friends and continue to visit them.

Margaret and Geoff, who lived opposite and Maisie and Ken a few caravans away.

Margaret's first child Mandy was born after Julie and we had some lovely times together and helped each other out during hard times.

The men did shift work and were on opposite shifts – so when they got paid, each would help the other, so Margaret and I could sort out the shopping. There used to be a mobile butchers and grocery van that came around on a Friday, where we would get extra's to tide us over. Our children were all of the same age and had lots of fun together. After a short time, we moved into a Council House at Dogsthorpe.

~

I used to be an Avon Rep and had a lot of customers so that brought a little cash in.

When both the children went to school I managed to get a part time job in Boots the Chemist.

In the year 1973, we moved from Peterborough and went into the Finance Business with a friend in Luton. We thought it would be a good opportunity to branch out.

The house was sold very quickly, and we first moved into a two bedroomed rented property, until we found a house that was suitable for us. The girls settled into school quite quickly and the schools they attended were very good.

We had an office in London, Oxford Street called Van Mel Associates.

After some time, Mike and Ray decided to move their office to Luton because the rent was too high in London and they spent a lot of time travelling.

Joan (Mike's wife) and I helped in the office and we both helped to look after the children. Unfortunately moving the office to Luton proved the wrong decision and the business suffered – that's when Ray and I decided to leave the company.

So, after two years, we moved house and came to Grimsby to live. At that time we were at rock bottom.

With hard work, we pulled through. We managed to buy a property (fortunately houses were a lot cheaper in Grimsby than Luton) which helped us stay on the property ladder.

Luton's own Caesar's Palace

Whilst living in Luton, my cousin Joan and her husband, Garth, came over to stay for the weekend.

In the evening we went to Caesars Palace Night Club to see Des O'Connor and we all enjoyed his performance. He was brilliant. As usual, we got our giggle hats on. Joan and I were so happy together.

One time when we visited Auntie Elsie and Uncle George we all went out together. Gordon, Derrick, Mam, Joan and myself. I would have been about 18. We went to the local club and had a brilliant time.

A chap that knew Auntie and Uncle invited us to his house for a night cap – but of course Joan and I, in fact all of us were a little extra merry – and was having a giggle. On entering his house – it was straight up the stairway and dark.

Silly Joan and I started to sing, 'Hernando's Hideaway … Ole!' and Gordon was trying to pair Mam off with the old chap. That made us even worse, but Mam wasn't having any of it. It was a laugh, no harm done.

Hairdressing

Ray and I's first house in Grimsby was on Little Coates Road. I continued to work at Boots, this was around Christmas time and I had a temporary post – they did then offer me a permanent position, which I was very grateful for.

After 2 years, working at Boots I decided to go to college for hairdressing and took my City and Guilds exam after training.

Mr Green the manager at Boots was very good as he allowed me to have time off to do my 2 and half days at college, for my Hairdressing Training.

This brings back memories of the girls I worked with, they were great and had lots of fun.

Remembering one day, Shirley was working on the till and a customer (a lady) came to ask for, what sounded like, 'freezer wheeze'. She asked me where it would be. I didn't know what the item was and all of a sudden it came to me; *'razor blades'*. I quickly helped the lady, but Shirley and I couldn't stop laughing all afternoon!

We had great teamwork at Boots Chemist and plenty of laughs and fun; working alongside Sue .E. and Sue. W. Especially when we worked in the Store room. Later I worked on the baby section and loved that too.

When I left to do my Hairdressing, they were all so very kind and generous with many gifts to help with my work and I am still using the cape when I cut my Husband's hair.

It was great. I loved my hairdressing over the years but at times, I missed the friends who I worked alongside, we were a good team.

I mentioned earlier that my Dad was a Barber and as early as I can remember I wanted to be a hairdresser. Although I do recall my Dad saying to me, not to do hairdressing as it wasn't healthy.

So, I suppose it deterred me, however by 35, I was a qualified Ladies Hairdresser. I was one of the first of a few to take it mobile; much to the annoyance of certain salon owners!

Mobile Hairdressing was just starting to be popular, much to the dismay of certain salon owners; there was a big write up in the paper against mobile hairdressers. I responded, as did other 'mobiles'. Although they tried to ban us – they didn't succeed, and it is still popular today.

I continued hairdressing until I was retirement age.

I would like to mention, a few of my clients whilst I was hairdressing as they are so important to my memories.

There was dear Mrs Fox, a delightful old lady, very clearly and precisely spoken. In fact, one could easily get the feeling that she was a cut above others, but no – she was the most kind and thoughtful person.

This one particular time, I was visiting another client in the building and had just given her a perm and Mrs Fox lived next door… I popped my head in and said, "See you tomorrow Mrs Fox." She asked me to come in.

So in I walked and she was sitting on the settee exercising her leg – it had a habit of going numb, which very often occurred which she liked to tell you (I think it was for reassurance).

I said, "Have you got your old trouble back again?"

"Yes June, I have."

"Never-mind." I said, "Keep up the good work." Making sure I kept a light-hearted approach to the situation…

Now Mrs Fletcher, the lady who I had given the perm to – she was a very bustling, busy little lady. She would do anything for anyone – she was really marvellous. Well into her 80's she was shopping, making cups of tea, organising bingo, knitting and dressing dolls. A thousand and one tasks (as the saying goes). I was never there very long before she would delight in making a cup of tea, and out would come the tray with a lovely crisp white embroidered tray cloth; using her best china, biscuits or home-made cake.

I served on average around 14 people in Stratford House, including some men. Now the men were all very proud of their appearance and loved the attention. I remember in particular, one gentleman, meeting in the corridor and he said very cautiously, "Hello are you the hairdresser?"

I said, "Yes! Can I help you…"

"Eh! Well yes, would you be kind enough to take some off this lot?"

Raising his hand to his head. Then he asked a question that took me aback, "Oh! And would you trim my moustache for me?"

So I quickly reacted, looking and thinking 'he looks very fussy and particular'.

"Oh yes certainly Sir." Considering I had never tackled one before all turned out well and he was one of my clients for many years, along with his wife.

~

I also served some people in Bovill House and many private houses. They were all lovely people and very grateful for my service to them.

There were two very special ladies in Bovill, one was called Mary and another called Edna. They were friends and there was always a lot to talk about and I always spent extra time with them.

It was a very special time and such a pleasure to be with most of my customers were with me around 15-20 years until I retired.

Scottish Dancing

Our second year in Grimsby, we decided to go to New Year's Dance at the Town Hall. That opened a lot of doors for us. We joined the Caledonian

Society and attended regular Scottish Dance classes on a Monday and Wednesday.

Ray and I went to lots of workshops and became Scottish Dancers.

Ray joined the Athol Pipe Band, now named the North East Lincs Pipe Band. We joined the holiday fellowship and had many happy years dancing and walking in Scotland, great companionship and met some lovely people who are still our friends and keep in touch.

Our friends who live in Scotland (Milngavie) we met at a Big Dance in Pitlochry 1989 and had many wonderful times with them and still do.

Remembering in particular when we danced at the Blair Castle. It was a wonderful atmosphere and the dance was called 'Trip to Bavaria'.

Well, we all went wrong and couldn't stop laughing! The people who were sitting out and watching said that it was worth watching – such a laugh.

Oh! They were a great crowd and wonderful memories.

Good Neighbours

We had a great neighbourhood, and everyone looked out for each other.

The Newcombe family was quite a big family but very well-mannered and clean. Gordon was a friend of Wilf, then there was Mabel, Sheila, Dennis and Barbara. Mrs Newcombe was a very small lady remembering her to always wearing a Pinny (Apron) which people did in those days and Mr Newcombe was a tall man and had a pleasant disposition. He always gave a nice smile and 'Hello'. Wilf never got into any mischief, like Gordon.

The Standley family lived opposite the Newcombes. Geoff Standley was Gordon's friend, and I used to have a soft spot for him in my early teens, he was such a well-mannered, quiet lad.

Geoff, Wilf & Gordon

Derrick married his sister, Ivy and went to live in Peterborough. Our children and theirs, Steve, Carl, Bruce and Glenn went to the same school and had many happy times together.

There was a very sad time in our lives when Derrick and Ivy's baby, Trevor (aged 6 months) passed away after a sudden illness while cutting his teeth. He was such a beautiful baby (as all babies are) and with that terrible tragedy, Ivy would go on to have many depressive moments. The death of a child never goes away, young or old.

Joan, one of Ivy's sisters married John and went to live in Australia in the 60's. On a trip to visit Ray's sister in Australia, we met up with Joan and

John and had a lovely time with them. Recently, Joan came over with her daughter and visited us for afternoon tea, along with her other sister, Annette, who lives in Grimsby.

The Hutton Family too lived in Convamore Road. Mrs Hutton, Kit, was a big friend of Mam's and use to go on holiday with her and Aunt Elsie and Uncle George. I believe she had three children; John, the eldest who I didn't really know, then Marjorie and the youngest Bernard, he would hang around with us in our early teens when All Saints Church was very active with Youth Clubs and different activities; Young People's Guild, C.L.B (Church Lads Brigade) Brownies & Guides.

The Hall family was well known to me, as I used to go to school with Maureen and we were good pals for many years until I moved to Birmingham. They always welcomed people into their home, and Mrs Hall was a lovely lady. Mr Hall was a very quiet man. David was the eldest and he married a girl in my class at school, Alison. Also, there was Kenny, Susan and Tony but I can't remember which order of age they came in. I believe Susan went abroad to live.

Next door to them, were the Tomlinson's, I believe they were related to the Halls, Joyce was the youngest who I knew quite well through

Maureen and there was Sheila, only knew her to say "Hello" – she passed away quite young. There was an elder sister, but I don't recall her name.

The Hopwood's lived next door to the Tomlinson's, but I only really knew Shirley she was two years older than me but there was a few of us used to hang around together. The Wrights, Pauline was my friend and she had 2 brothers, Brian and John.

The North family came next – Derek was the eldest then came Jean, Dawn, Sheila, Pat and Janet. Dawn was telling me recently that Gordon and a few of them (including herself) when the time was getting near Bonfire Night (Guy Fawkes) would go around raiding Bonfires to make their own bigger. I can't remember that, but I expect I would have known about it, most probably an onlooker. Dawn said she would be about 7 years old; all innocent fun.

The Wiseman family lived opposite the Halls, they were another lovely family. I didn't know everyone in that family; Margaret and Alan but have got to know Kath in my later years.

Gordon was a regular at the Gaiety Dance Hall where he met his first wife, Ricky. They had a long and happy marriage together but sadly Ricky passed away in October 1993.

A few years later he met and married Phyl. They were members of St. Nicolas Church and for a long time, members of the church didn't realise he was my brother. He was well liked and loved by everyone.

We were lucky to have such good friends in the neighbourhood, who were all loving and supportive.

The Family at People's Park, Grimsby

All Aboard

One day, Ray took me to Tysley in Birmingham. It was a lovely surprise as I thought we were going shopping with Dianne, his sister. But it turned out he had arranged for me to have a train driving lesson for my birthday!

Well, you could have knocked me down with a feather when he presented me with a card to have a lesson!

Feeling very anxious I said, "What have you bought this for?"

He replied, "I thought you liked Steam Trains?"

"Yes, but I didn't want to drive one!"

'Getting to grips with a Steam Engine'

Anyway, I suppose I sounded ungrateful but after the initial shock I proceeded.

First, I was introduced to the driver and given some overalls and a cap. And then was shown into the canteen where a mug of tea was given to me. Ray was allowed to stay. There were two groups and I was the only lady with two men.

We first went into the engine machine shop, which apparently is the oldest in the country. This was far too technical for me but very interesting.

Afterwards, we went onto the signal box, but I wasn't strong enough to pull the levers, so Ray did that part for me. I started my experience of driving on the shunter; the engine driver said, "Who's first?"

And of course, with me being the only lady, the two gentlemen said, "Ladies first."

So, after the driver gave the instructions he said, "Right off you go, you're on your own."

I had to go forward and then reverse, which I did twice. But on doing so the driver said, "You can see how far reversing you go? If you don't stop in time, I'll be off." And he laughed.

Anyway, I successfully carried the instructions out. When the men had finished their turn, we went for lunch and after we each took the defiant engine so far down the track and reversed back. I passed!

'I have always loved Steam Trains'

Ray's Broken Heart

In 1990, we were married 33 years when Ray became ill in town at the Royal Insurance company. Luckily, Gwen who worked there, immediately called for an ambulance. Ray called me at home to inform me he had taken ill.

Luckily, Lisa and Ian were coming to visit me (by chance) so they took me to the hospital.

The doctors told me a heart attack was imminent. With that, Ray had a cardiac arrest.

He was off work for 3 months following this and finally decided to take early retirement at 60.

We have enjoyed many wonderful holidays together and even travelled the many thousands of miles to Australia, Singapore, Thailand, Bali and Malaysia.

An extra special surprise for our 50th Wedding Anniversary was a cruise on the Queen Elizabeth II to New York; organised by Julie & Gary.

We then took the family to Finland for a holiday and that is a truly magical and special memory.

Ray was like a young boy again!

We have been fortunate to have had many lovely years together, travelling.

Our Legacy

I worked for a while, until I became pregnant which happened on my 21st birthday. Mam had come over and brought a celebration cake, so there were 2 things to celebrate.

At that time, Ray and I had moved from the flat into 2 Rooms, which belonged to an old lady from the Church. Ray, at the time, worked with a friend as a Mobile Greengrocery Assistant, then as an Assistant Caretaker at a Nursery. Ray's uncle was a caretaker of a school and knowing we would need a house, told Ray to apply for one and we moved into a school house in September 1958.

We had only been there about 2 weeks, when I had a haemorrhage and was taken into hospital and there I stayed until after our baby, Stephanie, was born January 29th 1959.

Although she was born full term, sadly she only lived 2 days, weighing in at 3lbs. I had Placenta Previa, which means the afterbirth had formed at the lower part of the womb.

It was a very traumatic time, from the beginning of my stay in hospital until I came out.

I was confined to the bed and in the first few weeks, I was sedated and didn't know the time of day, on morphine. Until I remember feeling so ill and thought I was dying and rang the bell and when the nurse came she alerted the sister and I heard her say "stop the morphine immediately."

I can't remember much after that until I was sitting up in bed, perhaps days later. It was a very austere environment and I was getting very depressed, instead of being happy, having a child. Luckily, times have changed now. My Mother came over to Birmingham, but she wasn't even allowed to visit me and the times for visiting were also very strict. My husband came to see me every evening after work; he had to travel on two buses and was only allowed half an hour. Considering I was in hospital over 3 months, there is not a lot I remember. There was one nurse called Nurse Tingle and when she listened to the baby's heartbeat, the metal trumpet they used would sink into my stomach, her head rested on it so heavily. I think she thought it was a head rest! -

I was in a private side ward for I don't know how long, until my Mam asked Ray to ask to have me moved. I wasn't even allowed to have Liquorice Allsorts (most probably for my own good) because of the salt. There's one meal I remember they brought me, it was one small piece of steamed fish with a spoonful of mashed potatoes.

Anyway, when I was put on the big ward, Mam used to send me Egg Custards without the pastry, which she made, they were lovely. Ray said he used to bring me Cheese and Onion sandwiches, but I can't remember them. I think I must have blocked a lot out of my mind.

My waters broke, which seemed many weeks before Stephanie was born, it wouldn't be allowed now because of complications.

I had to have her delivered by Caesarean section and went to full term. My husband held Stephanie once she was born and described her beautifully to me saying she was having a good look around.

The next evening the Night Nurse asked me if I had seen her and I replied that I hadn't. She said, "If you still haven't when I come tomorrow, I will take you to see her."

That day, when I was hoping to see her, sadly she had passed away. The first I heard of it was hearing Ray crying down the corridor as he was walking towards the wards. Thinking back, we were so naive, no questions were asked. They told my husband that they would see to all the arrangements and he didn't see her after she passed away. He wasn't allowed to know where she was buried; he came and said to me she would be buried with someone, so she wouldn't be on her own. And of course, being young and innocent, shocked and tired, no questions were asked. I just imagined her laying in a coffin alongside an old lady, so you can tell how naïve we were; not even a goodbye.

Over the years, I have thought a lot about it; how other families must have been in the same position (not knowing) and the heartache. The early years after losing Stephanie, we accepted everything what was said and bringing our other children up, we dismissed it and got on with life, but it never went away.

The day I came out of hospital was very difficult, not having our baby and having to pass the nursery down the corridor, it was heart-breaking, but I held together very well, and Mam was waiting to greet me with Ray. I can't remember getting home, but I know I felt very weak. But when we arrived home - what a welcoming sight! – a portable colour television and a warm glow of the open fire and Mam had prepared a lovely stew. A mixture of sadness and joy. Everything seemed so strange, being away for so long.

In the past 4 years, we have found (fortunately) where Stephanie was buried, in Birmingham and we have been to her graveside on several times.

She was buried alongside a sailor who gained the Victoria Cross, so although we still hurt, more so as we have got older, and had time to think, there must be thousands who have gone through the same trauma.

It is so much different these days. The internet showed us the way and a kind friend of ours, Carole, searched for us so we are very grateful. But having said that, there are a lot of questions not been answered. We just hold faith in our hearts that one day we will know. So, I say to parents, "never hold back, ask questions, you have a right."

~

Our second child, Julie, was born in 1961 on the 11th March and what a difference! The care was second to none. This was in Peterborough "The Gables". Although I had a long labour, I felt very confident because they were so attentive. A male attentive midwife was in attendance and he was so kind during the time I had to have forceps to help delivery.

Julie was born weighing 5lb14oz and was immediately put into an incubator because she was tired with having a long labour. Although I didn't hold her at that time, they did bring the incubator by my side before they took her in the nursery, so I could see her. All went well, and I was home within 10 days.

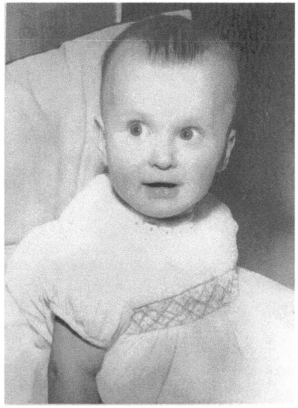

Julie

Julie would go to anyone! If anyone spoke to her in the pram she used to get so excited. Her little fingers and toes (if she hadn't got any shoes on) use to go ten to the dozen, but Lisa was completely different. You couldn't leave her outside a shop because if anyone looked in the pram, she wasn't a happy baby. In those days you weren't frightened to leave your baby outside. Even in Woolworths, you didn't walk around the store with your pram, it was left in the entrance, with or without the baby.

One time, we came to visit Mam, I'd been down Freeman Street shopping and on the way home I called in Hector Jacksons to get a bottle of milk and Julie was outside in her tan-sad pushchair just across the road from Mam's house. Got back to Mam's – talking – and all of sudden Mam said, "Where's Julie?"

"Oh no!" I ran across to Hectors and there she was… Just sitting there, so content, bless her!

She was a little angel.

Having said that, the time Lisa had her first hair cut at 1 year old, she was as good as gold. I took her to a men's hairstylist and she sat so still, in bewilderment, I believe. Of course, she could see herself in the mirror and I was by her side. He was a very nice gentleman who cut her hair and kept talking to her. No smile from Lisa though. I think she weighed people up, not easily taken in by charm.

She was a little gem.

~

When I was expecting our third child, Lisa - I went into the shed where we use to keep coal and a big moth settled on my arm which alarmed me as I don't like them. I knocked it off and went into the kitchen to tell Mam (we lived in Peterborough at the time and Mam had come over for a short stay) and I went all shivery and Mam said, "You silly girl, that baby will have a mark on its arm."

"Poppycock!" I said.

But when Lisa was born on the 20th March 1965, sure enough she had a birth mark on the same arm and same place as where it landed.

Lisa - you can see her birthmark on her upper left arm

It was just how a moth lands flat and it's grown with her and quite furry, downy hair on it.

So, I would never say "Poppycock" unless I was certain again, and may I say Lisa has had no qualms about it being there.

~

I gave birth to Lisa and was in the same Maternity Hospital and although I had to go in for rest because of high blood pressure the nursing was excellent, and I was comfortable, and Ray would bring Julie to the window to wave to me and all was well. Mam came over to look after Julie.

I went into labour but had to have a Caesarean section, because she was too big for me to deliver and her shoulder was in the wrong position. She weighed 7lb12oz.

Julie, bless her, adored her and was so excited when she came into the Hospital to take Lisa home, even though I had been away from her for 4 weeks and even after all these years, speaks of Lisa with great affection and love; she was never jealous of her baby sister.

~

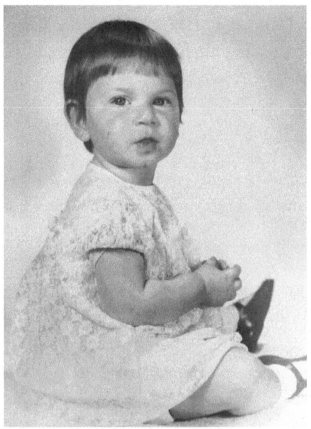

Lisa

Where we lived at one time in Ash close, Peterborough, we were fortunate to have lovely neighbours. In fact, we have always been very lucky wherever we have lived. When Lisa could walk she loved Kath and Doug and loved being in the garden but bless her, we found that she was very crafty and if she looked through the wire fence when Kath was working preparing lunch in the kitchen and Kath spotted her she would come out and out stretch her arms and off she'd go! Kath used to shout, "June, is it alright?"

So many a times she would go and have what they were having. But no sooner had she finished and wanted to be back to see where Mummy was. Lisa never left me out of sight very long, once she had her fill.

Julie & Lisa

Julie had a wonderful imagination and would play for hours, and once when we went out, she always had her imaginary cowboy with her, she would be about three and well! She would be so attentive with her imaginary friends that if I (not thinking) walked across the carpet, she would say, "Be careful Mummy, my cowboys are playing there!" She loved books, she would sit on my knee while I read to her and if I missed a line out I would soon know about it. She would say, "Mummy you missed some," and point to the words... Sometime I'd miss some on purpose, because I loved to hear her say it.

Now Lisa was completely different she never stays for long, she would bring a book to me but would soon lose interest. When she played in the garden with friend, every so often she would come in and say "Hello Mummy" making sure I was still around.

We bought Lisa a Go-Kart when she was about 4 and took her to pick it up from the toyshop which was only a short walk from where we lived. Of course, she wanted to ride in it without any help from us, "I can do it Mummy" but I hasten to add that I had to keep control of the steering which she wasn't very pleased about!

When we arrived home, straight into the garden, down the path, wobbling from side to side, she couldn't wait for Daddy to come home to show him. Julie was very good; Lisa didn't mind her sister helping.

Julie and Lisa started ballroom dancing but Lisa after a while didn't continue. They were both in the Orchestra at school; Lisa played the clarinet and Julie played the cornet.

We couldn't have asked for more loving daughters, who have grown into beautiful women. We are very proud of them both.

Grandchildren

Our grandchildren, Jade, Abbi and Liam, are kind and loving to us. Sometimes they laugh at what we do, and we have had lovely moments with them on holiday.

We looked after them quite a lot when they were young, especially on weekends, so we really have a close bond with them.

June & her Grandchildren - Abbi, Liam & Jade

Golden Years

Ray and I came to live on Wybers Estate in 1987 on my 50th Birthday. I remember standing in the kitchen looking out of the window - it was a glorious sunny day and I shouted to Ray through the window, "I feel as though I've been here forever." It just felt so right.

Our family are all close by and we see our daughters every week. The grandchildren stay in touch very regular and visit us when they can.

We have an allotment which Ray tends to and we reap the benefits of home produce.

Dancing, bowling and Ray playing in the Pipe Band keeps us busy and we have an active part at St. Nicolas Church, where we are fortunate to have a fantastic community of friends.

Love is all around us and spoken every day.

I have certainly lived, with my faith and love.

I have been truly blessed.

Forever known as, Dollipegs!

Acknowledgements

I wish to thank my two daughters Julie and Lisa for their encouragement to write my memoirs and the continued support of my Husband Raymond.

With a special thank you to Daisa & Co for their expertise, guidance and encouragement to believe in myself.

Bill & Derrick

Maureen, June & The Gang at Convamore Road

Ray & June holidaying in Ibiza

June & Ray visit Finland

Lisa, Ray, June & Julie

June & Ray

A Life of Love